IMAGES *of our Past*

HISTO
GLACE

CAROLE MACDONALD

NIMBUS
PUBLISHING

Nimbus Publishing Limited
PO Box 9166, Halifax, NS B3K 5M8
(902) 455-4286 www.nimbus.ca

Printed and bound in Canada
Typeset by Jesse Marchand
Cover design by Heather Bryan
title page photo: Glace Bay town hall, c. 1902

Nimbus Publishing is committed to protecting our natural environment. As part of our efforts, this book is printed on 100% recycled content, Enviro 100.

Library and Archives Canada Cataloguing in Publication

MacDonald, Carole, 1942-
Historic Glace Bay / Carole MacDonald.

ISBN 978-1-55109-689-6

1. Glace Bay (N.S.)--History. 2. Glace Bay (N.S.)--Biography. I. Title.
FC2349.G42M33 2008   971.6'95   C2008-905678-7

We acknowledge the financial support of the Government of Canada through the Book Publishing Industry Development Program (BPIDP) and the Canada Council, and of the Province óf Nova Scotia through the Department of Tourism, Culture and Heritage for our publishing activities.

Contents

Preface

C hipping off a bit of Glace Bay's fascinating history has been a challenging, exhilarating, and humbling experience. I came to the project believing that I knew so much about the town where my family has struggled, worked, and played since the mid-1800s, but even after two years of research, I have barely scratched the surface. I have confirmed my belief that Glace Bay is a town of strong, creative, and industrious people; a town that produced famous athletes, artists, labour leaders, politicians, and generations of citizens who have made significant contributions to the town and throughout the world.

It is unfortunate that the parameters of the Images of Our Past series limited the project to events prior to 1950, because it leaves out the considerable accomplishments of so many people. People like Nina Cohen, to whom we owe a debt of gratitude for the Miners' Museum and for the world-renowned miners' chorus, "The Men of the Deeps," or Allister MacGillivray, who before he wrote songs like "Out on the Mira," and "Coal Town Road," made his name in Nashville and toured with musical icons Tommy Makem, Liam Clancy, and John Allen Cameron.

Daniel Petrie showed the world one Glace Bay in his film, *The Bay Boy.* Sheldon Currie's book *The Glace Bay Miners' Museum* became the iconic film *Margaret's Museum.* He showed yet another side of the town in *The Company Store, A Novel,* which ran in theatres across Canada, as did *Lauchie, Liza and Rory.* His *Down the Coaltown Road* was nominated for the 2003 Dartmouth Book Award for fiction.

The "characters" in Glace Bay have long been the subject of the oral storytelling tradition and some have been chronicled in magazines and books, including *Big Cy and Other Characters: Pat MacAdam's Cape Breton.* Many will tell stories of Angus "Blue" MacDonald's creative use of the English language but as many will tell stories about the man's determination to work for the best interests of the community. Those who celebrate the successes of Glace Bay's Little League teams can thank Angus Blue for his dedication to the development of the sport of baseball in Glace Bay.

While I researched this book, I was constantly aware that most people in Glace Bay at the turn of the twentieth century had very little formal education, yet there was a culture of reading and of education. People read books, magazines, and newspapers and brought intelligent, critical judgments to the material they read. Along with well-known poets Lillian Crewe Walsh and Dawn Fraser, almost everyone learned, read, and wrote poetry. The number of bookstores in the town around the turn of the twentieth century suggests a literate society totally at odds with the image of a hard-drinking, brawling company town.

An apology to the people from Reserve, Broughton, Marconi Towers, Donkin, and Morien who have also contributed so much to the development of Glace Bay but whose history is not covered here. Early in this process, it became obvious that limits would have to be established and those were the town's boundaries of 1905.

It is my hope that this book will lead some readers to remember the joys, the struggles, and the people who made the vibrant town of Glace Bay, and perhaps encourage others to uncover more of the town's history, too much of which has disappeared in flames or under a wrecking ball—places like the pitheads, church spires, Senator's Corner, and Saint Paul's Church and its famous (or infamous) fence.

Thanking all the people who helped with this book leaves little room to describe the extent of their help, except to say their enthusiasm and encouragement made working on *Historic Glace Bay* a delightful experience. I sincerely apologize if I have left anyone out.

So, in no particular order: thanks to the wonderful staff at the Public Archives of Nova Scotia, Charles Hill at the National Art Gallery, staff at the Spring Garden Road and Glace Bay public libraries, the Miners' Museum, Isabelle Harris at the Town Hall Heritage Museum, Ann MacNeil and Jane Arnold at the Beaton Institute, and Theresa Smith at the UNIA.

Maureen MacNeil and Howard MacKinnon were incredible sources of information. Inglis MacAulay patiently searched for material and answered questions, as did Ernie Hennick at Nova Scotia's Department of Natural Resources and David Frank at the University of New Brunswick. Wally Crowdis, Frances MacDonald, and Jim Kennedy know almost everything about Table Head, the Stirling, and McKeen Street, while Don Burgoyne described every business on Lower Main Street in the 1940s. Raymond Goldman could always be relied on for information on Caledonia, the Jewish community, and the fishing industry.

Ken Walsh always had just the right photo an e-mail message away and Wayne Howie was always available to find a needed picture. Joe Steele entrusted me with his father-in-law Charlie Sweet's fragile scrapbook. Judy MacLeod provided photos and stories about her mother, Edie MacLeod. Kathleen Mackenzie at the St. Francis Xavier Archives found information on Reidville Street and Janet Burke had the photos. Family photos came from Don Beaton, Sue Edwards, Jim MacNeil, Amelia Burta Valley, Gloria Farmakoulis, Marie Bisson, and the late Chris MacIntyre. Alan Peddle of CJCB gave me permission to use

Cape Breton songs and Stewart Sheppard granted permission to use a Lawren Harris drawing. Acclaimed writer Sheldon Currie provided a needed push and Pat MacAdam offered material from *Big Cy and Other Characters*. Dr. Ron Stewart shared his knowledge of Dr. Leonard MacLean and Dr. K. A. McCuish.

Others who provided invaluable assistance include: Evelyn McDonald, Marguerite McNeil and the family of Marguerite MacDougall, Don MacMullan, Lydia Adams, Valerie Kinslow, Lorna MacDonald, David Ein, Shirley Chernin, Victor Jones, Rev. Kevin Grant, Cecelia Kelly, Herb and Linda MacDonald, Bernie Michalik, and Betty and Leonard Currie.

Introduction

Nicholas Denys, governor of Île Royale (Cape Breton), knew the importance of coal. In 1672, he toured the coast and wrote in his book, *Historique des l'Amérique*, published in France later that year, that there were "mountains of coal evident in cliffs in and around Baie de Glace." The French named the area "Baie de Glace" because the bay was encased in ice during the winter. The name was pronounced "Glass." ("Glass Bay" is the name recorded on a land request from a Mr. Blackett in 1818.) Because of this winter ice, the French chose the functional year-round port of Louisbourg to build

A. F. CHURCH AND CO. TOPOGRAPHICAL AND TOWNSHIP MAP OF GLACE BAY, 1864

a fortress to defend their territory in the New World. Coal was the fuel used to build and maintain the fortress, with much of that coal coming from the cliffs of Morien and Glace Bay. The earliest reference to European settlement in Glace Bay is of a mining village at what is now New Aberdeen. Established by the French, it became British property in 1748. It was burned by coal miners in 1752.

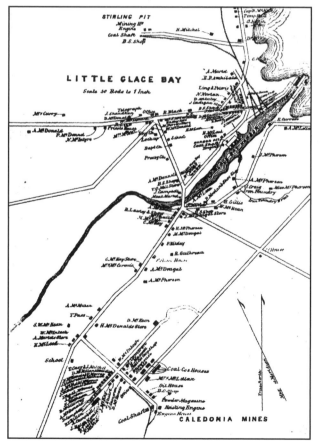

In 1758, the English gained final control of Louisbourg and destroyed the fortress. Demobilized soldiers petitioned for mining rights in the Glace Bay area, but were refused. The government in London discouraged coal mining and in 1766 issued a decree forbidding the gathering of coal in the area. King George III gave the mineral rights in Nova Scotia to his son, Prince Frederick, the Duke of York, in 1788.

The local government of the time begged England to allow it to grant mineral licenses, but to no avail. In time, Frederick, who had a penchant for fine living, handed the mineral rights over to a group of jewellers to satisfy a debt. The jewellers formed the General Mining Association (GMA) and began mining coal in Cape Breton. The GMA opened a mine in Sydney Mines in 1830 and shortly thereafter, opened a subsidiary at what is now Dominion. This was the only attempt by the General Mining Association to mine coal south of Sydney. That mine was short-lived, but its manager, Richard Brown, kept very careful records and wrote the first history of coal mining in Cape Breton, published in 1871.

Eventually the government of Nova Scotia, desperate for sources of revenue, managed to convince London to break the GMA's monopoly. Les Stephenson, a noted Dominion historian, records a Mr. Cadegan and a Mr. MacLeod opening a mine at Bridgeport in 1858. Other mines were opened at the Hub, the Sterling, Glace Bay Harbour, and Caledonia.

C. M. O'Dell reports in *Men and Methods of the Early Days of Mining in Cape Breton,* that

> the first mention of coal mining in Cape Breton by the Commissioner of Mines is in his report for 1864. In this report the commissioner expressed regret that no inspector of coal mines had as yet been appointed, and he was unable to give a detailed report of mining operations. He does, however, mention that there was a decrease in production of coal, as compared with previous years, "on account of a strike amongst the workmen."

In 1854, the British colonies, including Nova Scotia, worked towards establishing a free trade of goods across the U.S. border. This led to speculation in the mining industry and considerable financial investment in Glace Bay mines, increasing exports to the U.S. market. Money was raised in Sydney, North Sydney, and in the U.S.—local people either invested in or managed mines for outside interests. Unfortunately, the expected markets in the United States never materialized because the American government imposed tariffs to protect emerging coal industries in Kentucky and Virginia. To make matters worse, a general economic depression that started in the 1870s caused a decrease in production and many mines closed.

In 1878, Sir John A. Macdonald, Canada's first prime minister, implemented a national policy to encourage trade across the country. The policy consisted of high Canadian tariffs against American coal, and plans to open new markets in central Canada. While mining companies did well under this policy, miners themselves gained little.

The end of the economic downturn saw great manufacturing growth in Canada and a renewed need for coal. This coincided with a move in 1893 by Henry Whitney from New York and other investors from Boston, New York, and Montreal to consolidate the mines and build a steel plant. As a result, Dominion Coal Company Ltd. was incorporated in 1893. The original directors were Henry M. Whitney, Boston; Donald A. Smith, Montreal; Henry F. Dimock, New York; Hugh McLennan, Montreal; F. S. Pearson, Boston; Sir W. C. Van Horne, Montreal; Robert Winsor, Boston; W. B. Ross, Q.C., Halifax; Alfred Winsor, Boston.

COAL COMPANY STAFF, GLACE BAY OFFICE, c.1902

The Dominion Coal Company advertised for workers in Europe, and the Canadian government, which had sought out pioneers to settle the prairies, added the Cape Breton coalfields to their agenda. Now, immigrants bound for the prairies often left ships in Halifax and headed for mining opportunities in Cape Breton instead, supplementing the influx of Scots and Acadians from rural Cape Breton and the Irish and English from Newfoundland. Most Polish immigrants settled in Caledonia and worked in the Caledonia mine. Greek immigrants generally also settled in Caledonia, and Jews from Russia and Eastern Europe could be found in Caledonia, downtown, and at the Sterling. Black families, typically from the Caribbean, generally settled at the Sterling as well.

To accommodate the influx of people, the Dominion Coal Company built hundreds of new houses, mostly in Caledonia and New Aberdeen, in 1901. These supplemented houses built by previous mining companies in the mid-nineteenth century and acquired by Dominion Coal. By 1901, the area's population had grown from six thousand to ten thousand, and the various villages were incorporated into the town of Glace Bay. The town's first mayor was D. W. Burchell, superintendent of the coal company stores, which provided food, clothing, and mining equipment to the miners and their families.

Life in the mining community had not been easy before the arrival of the Dominion Coal Company, and if anything, things got worse afterward. With a massive influx of immigrants, the village was suddenly a boom town, and suffered from overcrowding, lack of sanitation, disease, and labour strife. Miners not only had to fight foreign-owned companies, but sometimes unions as well. Poor working conditions, irregular shifts, and companies concerned about profits at the expense of the miners—mostly young men with large families—were the norm. Although many families existed in conditions of near-starvation, it was the miners' wives who were often responsible for keeping their families and homes together.

Despite legitimate concerns about collusion between the union and the company, the miners' union, the Provincial Workers' Association (PWA), did succeed in implementing a system in which the company withheld money from miners' earnings to pay for services like doctors and schools. This method of deducting pay for social benefits was known as the "check-off system," and this system was later used to fund churches, hospitals, and a relief fund.

THE CHECK-OFF SYSTEM

Miners working for the Dominion Coal Company agreed to the check-off system as a condition of employment. Similar to the deductions that come out of paycheques today, the check-off system allowed the coal company to deduct money from employees' wages in return for funding doctors, schools, hospitals, relief funds, and later, churches. Outstanding bills at the company store were also settled through the check-off system.

Justice Emmett Hall, chair of the Hall Commission established to examine the state of health care in Canada in the 1960s, considered the Glace Bay colliery district the earliest form of mandatory healthcare insurance in the country. Tommy Douglas, the father of universal medicare, made several trips to Glace Bay to study the check-off system and implemented a similar program in Saskatchewan. It later became the template for the national medicare system.

Reference to the check-off program is first made in records of a PWA meeting in 1883, but there are indications that it existed much earlier, perhaps as far back as the 1830s. Len Stephenson, in his *History of Dominion*, refers to Dr. Marcus Dodd, employed at the International Mine in Bridgeport in 1866, to serve the areas of Bridgeport, Dominion, Lingan, and Morien. Wage deductions covered all medical procedures, services, and prescription drugs.

At the Sterling and Caledonia mines in 1888, miners paid forty cents each workweek for doctor's services. That entitled miners and their dependents to unlimited physician visits (including home visits), prescriptions and medications, surgical procedures and supplies, and hospital services. However, if a miner required medical attention not provided by the subscribed doctor and hospital, he was responsible for the fees.

Doctors hired by the company enjoyed a monopoly and a secure income, but worked incredibly long hours. A new doctor was required to sign up about one hundred potential patients before he could approach the company to join the system. If he did not reach the required threshold, any patients who had signed up with him would have to go back to their original doctor—not always a pleasant prospect. Usually, a new doctor assisted a practicing physician until he was able to gradually build up his own clientele. When the check-off system for doctors ended with the introduction of universal medical care in 1967, not all miners were pleased with the new system. The check-off was a cherished tradition. When a miner and his fiancée planned marriage, one of the most serious negotiations was the choice of a family doctor. Doctors became family confidantes and friends, and leaving a doctor's practice was often considered a personal insult.

After he visited the town in 1925, Lawren Harris, famous artist and member of the Group of Seven, painted *Miners' Houses, Glace Bay* and also published a drawing of a starving miner's wife and child in *Canadian Forum*. Harris also contributed several articles to Toronto's *Daily Star* about Glace Bay during the 1925 strike that gained the paper's support in helping raise money for the affected miners. Harris took considerable poetic licence when he described the desperation and hopelessness of the miners and their families, and there were some in Glace Bay who were embarrassed by Harris's efforts and ashamed of the widely held view of the town as a place of unrelenting poverty. Even Dawn Fraser, proud orator, poet, and publisher, distributed a pamphlet in 1925 urging citizens to rid Glace Bay of its poor reputation by petitioning for city status and a name change to Bay City.

While the image of Glace Bay changed little in the outside world, townspeople worked hard to build a solid community. There were those who made their mark internationally—war heroes like John Bernard Croak, who single-handedly captured a German machine-gun nest during World War One; Dr. W. L. MacLean, who pioneered work on blood transfusions during that same war; and Gus Edwards, who was instrumental in founding the Royal Canadian Air Force. In the arts, acclaimed writer Hugh MacLennan wrote several novels, including *Each Man's Son*, about Glace Bay at the turn of the twentieth century. Written from the point of view of the company doctor, MacLennan's depiction of Archie MacNeil, risking physical health and brain injury in brutal boxing matches, was not unlike the stories of many miners trying to break out of the misery and poverty of the mines by using their fists to benefit unscrupulous promoters.

Father Ronald MacDonald and Father C. W. MacDonald rallied miners to set up the first hospital in Glace Bay. Father John Fraser at Saint John's and Rev. McAvoy at the Baptist church worked tirelessly to help the poor during the 1909 and 1925 strikes. Much has been written about labour leaders like J. B. McLachlan, D. W. Livingstone, Dan McDougall, and others who led the fight for justice for the miners. National treasure, the late Nathan Cohen, although from Sydney, found a home for his political philosophies writing for the *Glace Bay Gazette*. Father Jimmy Tompkins, Mary Arnold, and Mabel Reed came to Glace Bay to help twelve miners build the town's first co-operative housing group. Lillian Crewe Walsh wrote the poem "The Lady of the Loom," and Elizabeth Belle Grant wove the words into the famous Cape Breton tartan. Marguerite MacDougall guided generation of children through local festivals, working with musicians destined for the international stage. MacDougall herself performed with national and international stars visiting the area.

After the 1947 strike, work in the Glace Bay mines achieved a degree of stability and prosperity that would last for a generation. Glace Bay began as a number of mining villages and grew into a community with a culture all its own. When the Dominion Coal Company took over the existing mines in Glace Bay and opened new ones, the sleepy village grew into the largest town in Canada at break-neck speed. Despite deep religious and political divisions, the people who lived in Glace Bay—who came from rural areas, from other provinces, and even from other countries—overcame their differences and used their incredible senses of humour to face hardship together and to fashion a unique culture their children carry with them wherever they go.

Chapter 1

People

HILLIER FAMILY, c.1900

A number of English and Irish immigrants settled in Glace Bay. Most of the Irish settled in Bridgeport and nearby Dominion. The Hillier family was among the first English families to settle in Glace Bay. They settled on one hundred acres of land on South Street. This photo was taken in 1900, one year after Mr. Hillier was killed in an explosion at the Caledonia mine, leaving his wife, Sarah, to raise a large family on her own.

Front row (left to right): George, Sarah (with Florence on her lap), Victoria, Daniel.

Back row (left to right): John, Ewan, Mary, Martha.

MacIntyre Pipe Band, c.1910

With the preponderance of MacDonalds and MacNeils, and MacKinnons in Glace Bay in the late 1800s and early 1900s, often the only way to distinguish them from each other was through nicknames. Nicknames could be based on ancestry, physical appearance, talents, occupations, or some reason that no one remembered or admitted to remembering.

Many nicknames originated from a man's work. One family gained their nickname because the family patriarch—although he worked hard all week—had so many deductions from his pay that he had only three cents left. As a result he and his children and grandchildren were known as the Big Pays. Leaky Joe put a new roof on a church and the first time it rained, the roof leaked. The Clocks' ancestor had one arm longer than the other. One man was called Fingers because he could play any stringed instrument. Biscuitfoot leaves plenty of room for speculation, unlike the Dancers, the Pipers, and the Fiddlers.

Tommy Michael Joshua's father was Michael, and his grandfather was Joshua. This was fairly clear, but if his father was Michael and his grandfather was Angus, it might be necessary to define who Angus was. Grandfather could be defined by physical appearance, so we might have Tommy Michael Red Angus. If grandfather had a particular occupation or lived in a particular place, Tommy could be Tommy Michael Angus the Boat (if he were a fisherman) or Tommy Michael Angus Big Pond.

Often ancestry and physical appearance were combined, as was the case for the son of Big Rory MacDonald, who married the daughter of Red Rory MacLean. The children all answered to either or both, and, in fact, had nicknames of their own, such as Buddy Big Red Rory. Big Mickey, Little Archie, Black Angus, Curley Joe were easy, as were the Shoemakers or the Bankers (the latter of whom fished off the Grand Banks). Then there were the Gaelic names that remain to this day, and the other nicknames whispered so the family would not be embarrassed by an unfortunate classification earned by an ancestor. In some cases, nicknames were so common that people forgot the real last names of some Glace Bay families.

While the dangers of mining meant many families in Glace Bay faced destitution when accidents claimed their husbands and fathers, others sometimes fared better. Susanna Lott, for example, married Michael "Black Mick" Sullivan at Saint Anne's Church in 1869. Black Mick was a merchant, a ship chandler, a tavern keeper, and a very large land and property owner in the Glace Bay area. The couple had thirteen children, four of whom died in childhood. After Michael's death in 1900, Susanna took charge of the family's real estate business, and according to oral history, became the harbourmaster. In 1901 she was supporting six children, her mother, and two grandchildren while successfully managing a business. Susanna Lott Sullivan died in Glace Bay in 1914.

One of Michael and Susanna's sons, Michael Thomas (M. T.), became a surgeon in 1901. He was also a coal company doctor in New Aberdeen and served as medical officer of health on several occasions. With others, he lobbied for clean water and sewage disposal in an effort to decrease child mortality in New Aberdeen. As well, Michael Thomas was Glace Bay's first marine doctor. He married Catherine MacLean (Cass) in 1902. Michael Thomas died in 1928. In 1930, Catherine moved to Halifax, where she became the first alderwoman in Canada (1931–1939).

During World War I, another son, Dr. John Lawrence Sullivan, joined the Royal Army Veterinary Corps and went to France in 1916. Returning with the rank of major, John Lawrence set up a veterinary practice—dedicated to treating horses—at the Sterling Yard, site of the former Sterling Mine. He was the first coal company veterinarian and even performed operations underground in the Glace Bay mines. He inoculated horses against diseases and invented an operating table and an ambulance for transporting them.

Along with Drs. M. T. and John Lawrence, Susanna's other surviving children were: Philip, a police officer in Boston; Caroline, who married Aubrey Stephens and settled in Dominion; Anastasia, who married John W. Devison and moved to the United States; Mary Josephine, who married John Abriel and moved to Halifax; Emma, who married Dr. Dan McNeil and lived in Glace Bay; Laura May, who married Dr. John A. Roy and settled in New Brunswick; and Bridget, a nurse who trained in New York and worked there until her death.

McPherson family, 1913

This photo was taken in May 1913 on Wallace's Road, New Aberdeen (the building may be what is today 136 Wallace's Road). The photo shows the Scottish McPherson family: Patrick, just home from his shift at the No. 2 mine; his wife, Isabella, with daughter Marjorie on her lap; Lionel, with a tricycle; Harriet, with a doll carriage; and Patrick and Isabella's niece, Nelly Almon.

By the mid-1800s there were roughly seventy-five thousand Scots in Cape Breton, outnumbering all other ethnic groups combined. Most immigrants left Scotland to escape economic, social, and political oppression, and some had earned land grants through service with the British military. When they reached Cape Breton, Scots had to tame the unfamiliar forests for housing, fuel, and cropland. Land along the water was taken first and provided decent agricultural land. Immigrants who arrived later were given poorer quality land with rocky soil that resisted most attempts at farming.

A crop failure and subsequent famine in the mid-1800s prompted an exodus from rural Cape Breton. Many immigrants left the province, while others moved to mining districts like Glace Bay, where Macs and Mcs became the dominant family names. By the late 1800s, Gaelic was a common language in Glace Bay—many other immigrants even learned Gaelic so that they could converse with the Scots in their native language. Soon, church services, house parties, concerts, and plays were held in Gaelic, helping to keep the Scottish language and culture alive. Unfortunately, many children of Scottish immigrants were taught in school that Gaelic was an inferior language, and as a result it was largely lost within a generation.

MEJDUK FAMILY,
c.1915

At the turn of the twentieth century the Dominion Coal Company offered free passage for people coming to work in the Cape Breton coal fields. Among those who responded were members of Jewish communities in eastern Europe, especially Poland, Lithuania, and Russia. Most wanted to escape economic and political oppression. Immigrants arriving around 1890 were mostly poor peddlers. Some began working in the pits, only to return to their original trades in the rural areas of Cape Breton.

The first synagogue in Atlantic Canada was built in Glace Bay in 1902. Many members of the Jewish community contributed to the construction of the synagogue before they even built their own homes. In the early twentieth century, there were also two kosher butchers in Glace Bay. Until the mid-1970s, a Hebrew school was held in the Talmud Torah building next door to the synagogue.

Jewish communities existed at the Sterling, Caledonia, and downtown. At one time there were thirty-five Jewish families along the Sterling Road, enough that the addition of another synagogue in the area warranted serious consideration.

**POLISH IMMIGRANTS,
c.1902**

Like most immigrants from Poland, Stanley Michalik and his family started life in Glace Bay at the turn of the century in one of the coal company shacks. These were huge warehouse-like buildings where families were separated by nothing more than curtains—there were no toilets, no running water, and no power. Because most Polish immigrants could not speak English and no one could spell their names, their lamps were numbered "Poland man #1" or "Poland man #2." Stanley and his seven sons all worked at Caledonia. Eventually many Polish immigrants bought land on Douglas Avenue and in other parts of town.

Sadie Bettens and her three children followed her husband to Glace Bay from Poland. Her husband (name unknown) worked in the mine and she took in washing. When they decided to build a house, they made their own bricks. Sadie didn't speak any English, so she had difficulty finding a Catholic school for her children to attend until a Jewish neighbour told her where it was.

MICHAEL BURTA,
C.1921

At age eighteen Michael Burta came to Glace Bay from Poland with five dollars to his name. Initially he lived at the Sterling, later marrying and building a house at the corner of Beacon and Argyle streets. He and his wife raised four children before she died, still a young woman. Michael then married a woman from Russia and the couple had two children. Michael's daughter Amelia recalled a warm, comfortable home where the family grew up on traditional Polish and Russian food. She also remembered family trips to the woods where her father collected edible mushrooms to take home and cook.

XIDOS FAMILY, C.1940

Many Greek immigrants settled the Glace Bay area. They were often men who planned on earning a decent amount of money and returning home to their families. However, most settled here and eventually brought their wives and children and other family members to Cape Breton. Some Greeks worked in the mines, mostly in Caledonia, but others opened their own businesses: restaurants, candy stores, and shoe repair shops. Tram conductors routinely dropped off newly arrived Greeks at the Dragates' Grocery Store in Glace Bay so they could receive assistance and shelter. George Markadonis donated a building site for the first and only Greek church in Cape Breton on Marconi Street in Glace Bay.

This photo is of the Xidos family. Front row (left to right): John, Laodiki, Irene. Back row (left to right): Catherine, Manuel.

Left to right: Chief Joe Francis, Mickey MacIntyre, Archie Forrester, Jack McVarish, George Thomas, Jack MacInnis, Mickey Morrison, Angus MacSween, William Wilton.

Despite the widely held belief that the Glace Bay police force was formed in response to abuses by the coal company police, it appears that when Glace Bay became a town in 1901, it already had an electrical department, a police force, and a fire department.

It's true that company police often overstepped their authority. During strikes the coal company often called on governments to send in provincial and federal troops to support the company police. The bills for transporting, housing, and feeding these troops were sent to the town government which, having refused to approve the need for their involvement, refused to pay them. The result of the attempt to charge the town for soldiers they didn't want or need is the basis for poet Dawn Fraser's "Send the Bill to BESCO."

The town force operated out of the town hall basement on McKeen Street. The jail was adjacent to the police station (and was also in the basement), and the town jailer lived on the third floor. Major crimes were few. While Glace Bay has a history of significant labour strife, there were only a handful of murders in the twentieth century. Most of the crimes the police force dealt with in the town's first eighty or so years were caused by alcohol—either fights resulting from overindulgent locals or citizens caught selling liquor illegally.

JOHN BERNARD CROAK,
c.1916

On August 8, 1918, John Bernard Croak of the 13th Canadian Battalion, separated from his section, bombed a German machine gun nest, taking the entire crew prisoner. Although he was seriously wounded, Croak managed to rejoin his platoon soon afterward. Shortly thereafter Croak's platoon encountered a second machine gun stronghold:

> Private Croak, however, seeing an opportunity, dashed forward alone and was almost immediately followed by the remainder of the platoon in a brilliant charge. He was the first to arrive at the trench line, into which he led his men, capturing three machine guns and bayoneting or capturing the entire garrison. The perseverance and valour of this gallant soldier, who was again severely wounded and died of his wounds, were an inspiring example to all.
> (*London Telegraph*, September 24, 1918)

Later that year at Halifax's Government House, Nova Scotia Lieutenant-Governor MacCallum Grant formally presented Mrs. James Croak of New Aberdeen with the Victoria Cross won by her son on August 8, 1918. Croak is honoured as Glace Bay's only Victoria Cross winner with a town statue and a New Aberdeen school that shares his name.

Alexander Bernard MacGillivray was born at Grand Narrows, Nova Scotia, on November 3, 1858. The family moved to Glace Bay and A. B. began working at the Bridgeport mine when he was thirteen. He worked in other mines before becoming a coal trimmer at Glace Bay Harbour, where he also became shipping superintendent. Then, in 1901, when Glace Bay was incorporated, A. B. was appointed stipendiary magistrate for the town, holding the position until his retirement in the early 1940s.

A. B. was widely known for his wit and quick judgment. One familiar story concerns a flippant young man who was found guilty of an offence. When A. B. fined him ten dollars, the accused was relieved. "That was easy," he said. "I've got that in my pocket." A. B. quickly added, "And thirty days in the county jail. Have you got that in your pocket too?"

When A. B. asked another man brought before him how he pleaded to the charges laid, the man said, "As God is my judge, I am not guilty." A. B. responded, "He isn't. I am. You are."

While generations of people in Glace Bay told stories about A. B., and while his courtroom was often filled with people waiting to hear his swift judgments and humour, others were not so impressed. Consider the tale of this anonymous resident who found himself in Magistrate MacGillivray's courtroom:

A. B. MACGILLIVRAY, C.1935

Come all you honest workers
    and listen to me
When you hear my story with
    me you'll agree.
Arrested for nothing and glad
    to admit,
One evening last week when
    coming from the pit.

Now a company policeman, a
  Man I know well,
And for to expose him
  The truth I must tell.
Whenever you see him you hear
  People say
There goes Dirty Danny—belongs
  to East Bay.

One evening of late coming
  Home from the mine,
As I walked along, some wood
  I did find,
It being my intention—the truth
  I must say
To use it to kindle a fire next day.

I had not gone far when I heard
  Someone shout
You're taking great chances,
  You better look out
I will have you arrested and a fine
  Make you pay
Remarked Dirty Danny—belongs
  to East Bay.

Without hesitation I threw the
  wood down.
And quickly departing for home
  I was bound
But two evenings later I'll have you
  to know,
MacAuley came after me and I
  had to go.

Now when I did appear his honour
  did say
Now you're charged with stealing
What
  have you to say?
I pleaded not guilty but it was
  no good,
Dirty Danny, he swore I was caught
  with the wood.

I tried to explain but I saw it
  was no use.
His Honour remarked "Sir I
  want no excuse.
You will pay $7.50 or else put
  up bail,
Or the rest of the night you will
  spend in the jail."

Now, times being hard and my
  Dollars but few,
I has to consider just what
  I could do.
To pay $7.50 was sure hard on
  me—
I will never forgive him, his
  Honour A. B.

Now Dirty Danny, your friends are
  but few,
And what I hear men say if
  you only knew
You'd be so ashamed you'd decide
  on a cruise
And go back to East Bay and
  hide in the spruce.

Now one thing I'll mention, I
  almost forgot,
I hope, dirty Danny, hard luck
  is your lot.
And everyone slight you, wherever
  you be
Just to remind you what you
  did to me.

Now to conclude, and to finish
  my song:
The truth I have stated, you'll
  find it's not wrong.
I hope to be even—if I live—
  some day
With my "friend" Dirty Danny
  —belongs to East Bay.

(From the Sweet family scrapbook provided by Joe Stee

HAROLD "GUS" EDWARDS, 1942

Harold "Gus" Edwards was born in England and moved to New Aberdeen in Glace Bay at the age of ten. He went to work as a trapper boy at fourteen in the coal mine where his father and brother worked. (Trapper boys worked underground in mostly solitary conditions in the dark, opening and closing doors to allow passage for horse-drawn boxes of coal.) Like most boys at the time, Gus worked ten hours a day, six days a week. He eventually became an electrician with the coal company.

Edwards had a lifelong passion for learning. He would get up at 3:00 A.M. to study for three hours before going to work. His mother made sure he and his brother were exposed to good literature, classical music, and opera. As a child, Edwards could repeat all of Shakespeare's sonnets by heart.

In 1915 Edwards joined the Royal Naval Air Service. He was shot down over Germany in 1917 and spent the rest of the war in a prisoner of war camp. Here his passion for learning served him well. During his incarceration he taught himself French and German. In 1920, Edwards joined the Canadian Air Force, which became the Royal Canadian Air Force (RCAF) in 1924. In 1942 and 1943, Air Marshal Edwards commanded the RCAF's overseas operations. He retired in 1944 as one of only three air marshals in the RCAF.

Glace Bay men and women made other significant contributions to the Allied war effort in both World War I and World War

II. One group, little known in Canada today, is the Glace Bay tunnellers. During World War I, the Germans made great advances tunnelling under Allied positions until Britain called on members of the Commonwealth to send their miners to fight this underground war. Miners arrived from Canada, Wales, Britain, and Australia. Several books and articles single out the achievements of the Canadians, and of those Canadians the miners from Cape Breton, mostly from Glace Bay, stand out.

Captain Roy Spencer was photographed at the time receiving congratulations from King George V. Cecil North, a surveyor at the Caledonia mine, was promoted several times and his exploits at Messines are recorded in books on the subject of tunnelling in World War I.

Lieutenant George Morely, Major Gillis Macaulay, Sergeant Dan Lynk, Dan Cameron, and well-known union leader Dan MacDougall were among the Glace Bay men who dug tunnels under enemy positions to either establish listening posts or blow them up. A 1918 article says that in an international competition for "sapping" (setting explosives), a team from the Caledonia mine beat all competitors, establishing a new record. According to the same article, "a dozen or so of the men of the No. 1 Tunnelling Company won medals and distinctions," but the article records no other names.

In a December 26, 1918, article, Sir Douglas Haig, in charge of Allied operations in France, noted the important contribution of miners in the war: "Before they leave the country, I wish to convey to… all ranks of tunnelling companies both imperial and overseas, my very keen appreciation for the fine work done by tunnelling companies throughout the last four years. At their own special work, mine warfare, they have demonstrated their complete superiority over the Germans."

**EDIE MACLEOD,
C.1940**

For decades, Edie Roy MacLeod was an enthusiastic chronicler of social life in Glace Bay. Born in 1912, Edie attended the first Central School on York Street and remembered the large 1919 fire that sent students into church halls and other locations to continue their education.

When she finished grade eleven at the age of sixteen, Edie planned to enter nursing school, but her mother's sudden death led her to get a job to help her father and younger sister. Her first job was at Samuel's Meat Market and she later worked at the Dominion Store on Commercial Street. Charlie MacLeod (of MacLeod's Bookstore) suggested she apply for a job he knew was coming up at the *Glace Bay Gazette*. She did.

Edie carried a large typewriter from the office to her home to practice typing. She carried it back the next day and got the job, where she pounded out stories using only two fingers on each hand. She worked at the *Gazette* until signing on as a correspondent for the *Halifax Herald* in 1941. She also worked for the *Cape Breton Post* where, although her job was to collect ads and write a column about those stores that committed advertising, Edie was able to sneak in some gossipy tidbits that made the column popular. The job lasted until the *Courier* set up shop in Glace Bay. Starting with pictures from her own album, she suggested and edited the "Down Memory Lane" centre spread that attracted subscriptions from as far away as New Zealand. She also edited the rest of the paper. At the same time, Edie was raising three children and writing for the *Highlander*, the *Atlantic Advocate*, and *Cape Breton Magazine*.

Edie also had an eye for photography. It was not unusual for well-known photographer Lal Shedden to call Edie when he was over-booked and ask her to grab one of his cameras to cover a local event. Along with skiing (she stormed a ski hill for the first time at the age of fifty-eight) and skating (both ice and roller), she was the original member of the York Street Extension Garden Club and recommended the calendula as the floral emblem for Glace Bay.

She received, among other awards, the Queen's Jubilee medal. When she was invited to meet Prince Charles and Princess Diana on board the *Brittania* in Halifax Harbour, she asked them without hesitation when they were going to visit Cape Breton.

The name on the store was Mendelson's, but nearly everyone called it Sammy's.

Sammy Mendelson was the oldest son of Russian Jewish immigrants, both of whom died young, leaving Sammy and three younger siblings an empty candy store in the midst of the Jewish community on Glace Bay's Sterling Road.

During strikes and slowdowns, Sammy, like many other merchants in town, offered credit to miners and their families, carrying the debt on his books until it could be repaid. Some families never paid their debts, but most did and remained loyal to retailers like Sammy who helped them in hard times.

If Sammy didn't have what a customer wanted, he would go out of his way to find it. One Christmas in the 1940s, a woman looked all over town for a doll carriage for her daughter, to no avail. On the way home, she stopped at Sammy's for milk and told him of her fruitless search. That night, Sammy arrived at her door with the doll carriage. Not only had he found one in Sydney, he had the store owner hold it for him while he drove in to get it.

Every Sunday morning, especially when the weather was bad, Sammy's car was on the road, driving people to churches downtown. Anyone in the neighbourhood who wanted a job had it. Whether it helped young people get through school or helped a family in need, there was a job at Sammy's.

Sammy died in 1989. Still, ask most people in Glace Bay if they remember him and you will get a nostalgic smile and an enthusiastic response: "Oh, of course I remember Sammy. He was a great man. I remember when…"

Chapter 2

The Mines

BLOCKHOUSE AT WINDSOR, C.1905
(THE BLOCKHOUSE PICTURED HERE IS SIMILAR TO THE ONE AT TABLE HEAD.)

The French at Louisbourg established a mine at Table Head in the early 1700s. At that time, Table Head included the Hub and at least part of New Aberdeen. The 1748 treaty of Aix-La-Chapelle ceded Louisbourg to the English. Miners at Glace Bay signed a pledge of allegiance to the English as well.

But the English-French conflict was not over. Anticipating a French attack, a garrison of some fifty men was sent to defend the village. Colonel Hobson, the English governor of Cape Breton, sent to Maine for supplies to build a blockhouse (similar to the one pictured). The garrison, commanded by Lieutenant Rhodes, had barely finished building the fort when the French attacked.

In one version of the attack, the French commander demanded that Lieutenant Rhodes surrender the fort. Rhodes considered the demand, but in the end, announced that he could not in good conscience surrender. The French then took soldiers, miners, women, and children, and loaded them on boats bound for Scatarie Island, not far from Main-à-Dieu. In another version of the attack, the French burned down the miners' houses, captured three ships, twenty-four men and women, an English officer, and an English soldier. Colonel Hobson reported to the Duke of Newcastle that those captured were then taken to Scatarie Island.

In any event, the Table Head mine was reopened when the French regained control of Louisbourg. In 1752, the mine was set on fire by "disgruntled miners." The fire burned for several years. Thus, the area of Glace Bay at the end of Eleventh Street became known as Burnt Head, where remnants of that fire can still be seen in the cliffs behind Saint John's Church.

By the mid-nineteenth century, coal mines were opened in Bridgeport, the Hub, the Roost, the Sterling, the Harbour, and Caledonia.

MINERS AT THE HUB, c.1890

This photo was taken in the vicinity of the Black Diamond Oval, a famous horse-racing venue of the late 1800s and early 1900s.

The houses in the background of the photo were built for employees at the Hub mine, which was opened by Archbold and Company in the early 1860s after the General Mining Association lost its lease on the mineral deposits. The men with the horse and cart are carrying coal, possibly from the nearby Hub mine, but most likely from one of several bootleg pits in the area. Then, as now, the province owned all mineral resources and only mines licenced by the province were legal. Although bootleg mining was illegal, people in Glace Bay relied on such mines for their coal. To this day, gathering surface coal is still, technically, illegal.

Later in the nineteenth century there were attempts to mine the old
French workings near Burnt Head. Dug into the cliff from the shore,
the Roost Mine began operating in 1857 near the old French mine.
A wharf was built and scows transported the coal to larger vessels
that travelled to markets in Halifax. Later, the mine was moved to an
area close to Burnt Head, but it had a weak roof and was abandoned
in favour of access at Shag Roost, so-named for the number of shags
(cormorants) that nested there. The mine opening was on the coast
between what are now Hill and Hay streets. The Little Glace Bay
Mining Company built houses there in 1861.

Patrick Cadegan and Rev. Hugh McLeod opened a mine at
Bridgeport in 1858, which they then sold in 1863 to the International
Mining Company (IMC), an American consortium. The first workings consisted of a level driven from the shoreline and a slope driven
on shore. Production at the mine was sporadic until 1870, when the
main shaft at Bridgeport was sunk to a depth of ninety-six feet. The
coal was transported to the shore by rail cars and hand loaded onto

waiting boats at a small wharf at Deadman's Cove. The IMC also constructed a railway from Bridgeport to the port of Sydney.

From the beginning, control of coal resources was largely in foreign hands, and the American-owned IMC was no exception. When Rev. Richard John Uniacke travelled to Glace Bay around 1864, he marvelled at the stars and stripes proudly waving from a staff at Bridgeport.

The first Caledonia mine opened in 1864. It was, at one time, owned by Alexander Graham Bell's father-in-law, Gardiner Hubbard, an attorney from Boston who installed a telephone from the surface of the mine to the coal face, making it the first commercial telephone in Canada.

The company tried to maintain a wharf at the outlet of Glace Bay Lake by building a railway across the sandbar to an artificial harbour. The wharf was in operation for ten years but maintaining the harbour was a constant battle against nature. Finally, the company arranged to pay the Little Glace Bay Mining Company to use the wharf at Glace Bay Harbour, itself formed by digging out Renwick Brook as far as the Commercial Street Bridge.

This Caledonia mine closed in 1892. It later reopened and was absorbed into the Dominion Coal Company (DOMCO), where David McKeen became manager. (McKeen also owned the company store and later became lieutenant-governor of Nova Scotia.) On June 6, 1899, eleven men were killed in an explosion likely caused by a spark that ignited methane gas. It was the largest number of mining fatalities in the Glace Bay district to that point.

In 1927, twenty-eight years after the devastating explosion, the Caledonia mine won an award for being the safest mine in the Dominion Coal Company coal fields. The picture of the award hung in the company office for thirty years as a reminder for employees of the need for safety.

In this photograph, mine manager Mr. Dinn sits holding the trophy. Front row (left to right): William Attwood, John David MacMullin, Alex Munroe, Ted Higgins, Malcolm McKinnon, Cyril Dawe, John R. MacDonald, Bill Shaw, William Dillon, John Rankin, Archie MacDonald, Murdock MacDonald, Richard Wilton, Joe Hest, and Hector MacDonald. Back row (left to right): Tom Scott, John J. MacLean, Alex MacKinnon, Archie Nicholson, John Murdock Morrison, Tom Allan MacDonald, Tom Nicholson, Ronald MacInnis, and Norman Morrison.

STERLING PIT, C.1870 The Sterling mine, which operated from 1863 until 1896, was located at the intersection of the Sterling Road and McKeen Street. This location later became the Sterling yard, the central depot for storing goods for the other mines, and was the site of a veterinary hospital dedicated to looking after pit horses.

Mines also opened at the north side of the harbour near the Commercial Street Bridge (the Harbour mine) and at the Hub. Reports claim that the Harbour mine yielded little until new shafts were driven at the Sterling site in 1872. The two mines were connected underground in 1879 so that coal could be transported to the newly constructed Glace Bay Harbour. Coal from the Hub and the Roost mines travelled on a raised rail line along the west side of North Street to the harbour. When construction of the harbour was completed, coal from the Archbold mines was loaded on the north side while Caledonia coal was loaded on the south. There were also attempts to join the Sterling pit with the underground mine at Bridgeport, but this was never completed. Many company houses built near the Sterling mine still stand on Minto and North streets, and on Devison's Lane.

In 1893, the Dominion Coal Company negotiated a ninety-nine-year lease on the coal fields south of Sydney Harbour. At the same time, it invested in a steel plant in Sydney, giving the company a local market for its coal. Company-owned rolling stock and ships transported coal to other markets.

At New Aberdeen, the No. 2 colliery (which included No. 9 and later No. 20) was known as "the big producer." Caledonia was expanded but smaller mines—including the No. 3—that had been absorbed into the Dominion Company were worked for a short time and then abandoned.

CALEDONIA COMPANY STORE, 1902

Goods at the company stores were expensive, and the mining communities were a captive market, at least until private competition arrived. The stores carried an extensive array of goods, including farming equipment, mining clothes and materials, food, furniture, and family clothing. Miners were not forced to purchase at the company store, but with little or no cash, options were limited.

In the early years, the mines usually closed in the winter. Single men often went back to their rural communities and returned to the mines when crops were planted in the spring. But once they married and had families, miners were less mobile. As a result, when the mines were not working, married men stayed in their company houses and continued using the company store, piling up debt that had to be paid when the mines started working again.

Despite the hardships visited upon the miners and their families by the company stores, it was a point of pride if one's son or daughter got a job there. The work was clean, above ground, and required education. By the start of the twentieth century, most of the employees at company stores were women.

The government of Nova Scotia owns the mineral resources through-out the province, so in Glace Bay, where pockets of coal are readily available, it was, and is, illegal for anyone to collect it without a license. Although never proven, it has been a long-held suspicion in Glace Bay that a few outhouses and garden sheds here and there might actually have been entrances to bootleg mines.

Even during the Depression and other times of hardship, it was ille-gal for anyone pick coal from beaches or along train tracks or in their own backyards. Even today people have been known to report others gathering coal illegally. Nevertheless, people still bootlegged coal, and in some cases it was even considered necessary. One unsubstantiated story located a bootleg mine under a downtown church, where, during the 1925 strike, it was alleged that a minister dug coal for the needy in the community.

In the 1930s the *Glace Bay Gazette* reported that members of the UMW Victory Local union appealed to the government to stop pros-ecuting young men for bootlegging because destroying their livelihood forced them onto a tenuous welfare system. At the time, there were few jobs, the coal company was not hiring, and the perceived wisdom was that by bootlegging, these young men could provide for themselves and their families. The union's position was that dynamiting the openings to bootleg mines or arresting the bootleg miners—the practice of the police at the time—served no useful purpose.

The coal company sometimes tried to turn a blind eye to bootleg-ging, but in 1948 the RCMP mounted a concentrated drive against bootleg mines. The Dominion Coal Company issued a warning to the public that persons purchasing illegal coal could be charged with receiving stolen goods. A Sydney newspaper reported that bootleg coal found a ready market during the strike of 1947, but because bootlegging had gained the status of an industry, an "intensive drive against such mining is essential."

And while deliveries of legal coal were available to those men employed by the coal company, for many others, bootleg coal was the only option for heating their homes. Today houses and roads are occasionally undermined by bootleg mining activities, although these cave-ins are usually the result of very old or very shallow mines.

MINER WITH PIT HORSE, c.1955

Until mines became fully mechanized, miners relied on pit horses to help them transport coal. The horses saw daylight only during the miners' vacations when they were brought up out of the pits and allowed to roam the fields near the collieries. At one time horses from the No. 20 colliery were corralled in a field at the end of what is now Reidville Street. Later they were kept in a field bounded by the No. 20 colliery, the Sterling, and Table Head. Horses from Caledonia were kept in a fenced, grassy field near the No. 4 pithead. As a result, miners' vacations were memorable for many in Glace Bay who would go to feed the pit horses.

Most miners treated their horses well, since a difficult horse made for difficult work. Miners would even visit their horses in the field during vacation. A call or a whistle from a miner who worked with a particular horse would bring the animal to the fence to be fed or petted. If someone at the fence called to one of the horses and it shied away, it was a message to all that the horse was not being treated well underground.

MINERS' COTTAGES, c.1935

This photo shows a row house built in the mid to late 1800s, before the amalgamation of the coal companies. While most houses were single family or duplexes, there were units of four or more at Bridgeport, the Roost, the top of Minto Street, and Caledonia. Each mining community had a school, churches, a company store, and eventually, a volunteer-built and -operated athletic club, often with a skating rink attached.

From 1860 to 1880, the Roost expanded, as did areas around the north side of the harbour, the downtown, Caledonia, and the Hub. The houses built at the Hub during this time bear a strong resemblance to those in the outports of Newfoundland, so it is believed that a Newfoundland builder constructed them. It is likely some of the houses at Bridgeport date back to the International Mining Company in the mid-1800s.

Along with the new houses built by the mine owners, from the late 1880s to the early 1900s many houses were also brought overland from the defunct mining areas of Port Morien and Broughton. Houses were also moved from Lingan when the mine closed there in the mid-1800s, and some of the Lingan miners who came to work at the Roost may have brought their houses with them.

DUPLEX HOUSES, 1945   These duplex houses, built in 1901, were part of a building boom in Glace Bay. The majority of these houses were built in New Aberdeen and Caledonia, but they can be found in other areas as well.

The Dominion Coal Company reorganized its mines and advertised for more workers in Europe at the turn of the century. The increase in the workforce soon meant a housing crisis in Glace Bay—which led, in turn, to rapid construction of new buildings. Practically overnight, two new "towns" appeared in 1901: Dominion No. 4 (Caledonia) and Dominion No. 2 (New Aberdeen). Stewart McAulay, a historian in early Glace Bay, wrote that two hundred new houses were built in Caledonia on well-planned streets, and the community had a public square, churches, and a public hall. The original Caledonia area also had its existing housing expanded by forty additional double houses. Two hundred new houses were also built at New Aberdeen, where according to McAulay, there was a hospital, good roads, and a large park. None of the new houses had basements or bathrooms but they were sturdily built.

Most of the miners and their wives were young and had large families. Many grew vegetables in their yards and some kept cows, pigs, or chickens to feed their families and to supplement what was available at the company stores.

With the explosion of immigration, overcrowding was the norm, although many private homes also took in boarders. The overcrowding and lack of proper sanitation led to an untold number of deaths from communicable diseases. During one week in mid-August 1924, Campbell and Warden Undertakers buried twelve children, while Curry and Son buried no less than twenty. On August 22 of that year, a two-year-old girl from New Aberdeen died at St. Joseph's Hospital from cholera infantum.

Medical officers reported that diphtheria epidemics in New Aberdeen that continued into the 1930s were due to polluted water. Cecelia Kelly recalled scooping water from horses' troughs to take home in New Aberdeen. In fact, it was not until the Depression of the 1930s and its various make-work projects that most houses in the area had sewage hookups.

The word "shacks" seems to have several meanings in Glace Bay. In New Aberdeen, it referred to accommodations pieced together by groups of men who either could not find other lodging or who were saving all their money to bring their families to Glace Bay. In Caledonia, the company built "shacks" that consisted of large open spaces where families crowded, separated only by curtains and without sanitary facilities. Early histories of Glace Bay refer to rooming houses constructed by the company for single miners as "shacks." These boarding houses were built because hundreds of men arrived in Glace Bay each day looking for temporary work in the mines. Each boarding house accommodated seventy-two men, two to a bed.

"Summer miners" came mostly from rural Cape Breton. Stephen Hornsby writes that these miners could have made one hundred dollars for five months of work. Much of that money would have gone to room and board, but the twenty or thirty dollars remaining would be a boon to subsistence farmers in rural Cape Breton. Many of these summer miners met their future wives in Glace Bay and stayed to build lives and families in the community. Wages were low, but so was rent at company houses. Many families were large and often got caught in the cycle of debt to the company for rent and goods from the company store. Living in company houses could prove detrimental in times of labour strife. Repairs were few and the miners themselves refused to improve company property since every mining community had seen families evicted when men challenged the company or died. Joan Latremoulle notes in *Pride of Home* that company houses offered cheap rent and the rent could not be raised because the pay was low. Those who owned their own houses did not always fare better. Many had mortgages that tied them to the mining company.

REIDVILLE STREET,
c.1939

Not all miners lived in company houses. Some built or bought their own homes while others entered into a new type of co-operative housing where one mortgage covered several houses. In 1939, while Father Tompkins, Mary Arnold, and Mabel Reed started working with a group in Reserve to establish a co-operative housing group, they were also working with a group in Glace Bay, where sixteen families began learning co-operative philosophies, how to build houses, and how to hold co-operative mortgages. Twelve committed themselves to building a co-operative housing group at Reidville Street (named for Mabel Reed but with a change in spelling).

The children of the twelve Reidville families lived under the scrutiny of twenty-four pairs of eyes. But they had the benefit of attending the new Sterling School with other children from Celtic, Jewish, Black, Newfoundland, and European backgrounds and living near as cosmopolitan an area as any big city can offer. While the people of Tompkinsville, in nearby Reserve Mines, gained fame as the first successful co-operative housing group in Nova Scotia by paying off their mortgage first, Reidville was a close second. Others soon followed, including the Churchill Centre co-op at New Aberdeen.

Not all members of co-operative housing groups were miners. At both Reidville and Churchill, steel plant workers, taxi drivers, and town employees were part of the group. Two original members of the Reidville co-op were boxers Stevie "Kid" MacDonald and Joey Burchell.

In the downtown, on Chapel Hill, South Street, and in pockets of every community there were, of course, privately owned houses. Built in 1901, this house on King Edward Street was the home of the Curry family. The owner, Will Curry, was a contractor who built the coal company houses at Caledonia and New Aberdeen, and he also founded Curry's Funeral Home. The business passed to his son Charles, who with his children moved into the Curry home. The house later became a bed and breakfast called "Will-Bridg," named for Will Curry and his wife, Bridget.

Other privately owned homes housed the families of company officials or members of the professional class. For many years, the superintendent of mines lived at Sterling House, a large house between Minto and North streets that was later turned into an apartment building. The homes of Magistrate A. B. McGillivray and film director/producer Daniel Petrie still stand on Main Street, and just up the street, Jack MacRea's Afton Hall is now Curry's Funeral Parlour.

Another house made famous by its occupant was Canadian author Hugh MacLennan's home at Caledonia Crossing. The house was built by Hugh's father, Dr. Sam MacLennan. It had four fireplaces and a spacious nursery running the total length of the upstairs on one side, where the windows were fitted with protective bars so that children would be safe even when the windows were open. The MacLennans moved to Sydney Mines and in 1920 the Dominion Coal Company bought the home for the manager of their Caledonia Colliery, John Casey, who was the first local man to become a mine manager.

Lots of help was available in those days, so a gardener was available to look after the expensive vegetable and flower gardens and the numerous apple, cherry, and hazelnut trees on the grounds. Household chores were done in the morning so that the afternoons were as free as possible for socializing. In fact, one of Mrs. Casey's daughters remembers her mother saying that she was glad to return to the former home on Casey's Lane to get some rest.

The MacLennans planted many trees on the property and they were known to come back and walk through the grounds and even to take slips of the trees they had planted during their residence there.

Later the house was occupied by J. R. MacNeil, manager of the No. 11 mine, and his family, and subsequently by Murray Wilton, who with his wife, Margaret, raised ten children in the house while maintaining the extensive vegetable and flower gardens. The house was sold in the 1950s and converted to apartments before it was demolished to make way for Newsom Church.

Chapter 3

The Strikes

ARMY OFFICERS AT NO. 3 COLLIERY, 1909

From the 1700s to the 1900s, labour strife was part of the fabric of Glace Bay. The first known labour strife in Glace Bay coal mines occurred in 1752 when disgruntled miners set fire to the French mine at the end of what is now Eleventh Street (the area subsequently became known as Burnt Head). Poor working conditions and low, often inconsistent pay led to strikes throughout the 1800s. The

1888 Royal Commission on Labour and Capitalism heard miners tell of the hardships they and their families faced. Those who could leave, did. But many others had come to Glace Bay because of difficult economic conditions elsewhere. Many had little education; they married young and had large families, often living in poor company houses and becoming indebted to the company store. They couldn't leave. Fighting for their rights became the only option.

The miners' union—the Provincial Workman's Association (PWA), formed on the mainland of Nova Scotia in the late 1800s—gained some concessions from coal companies, and these concessions spread to the mines in Glace Bay. The concessions included safer working conditions and a union-appointed check weighman who was paid through the check-off system. Because men were paid by the ton for coal they loaded in boxes, there had long been a concern among the miners that the check weighman, hired by the company, would cheat the miners by claiming coal boxes weighed less than they actually did (as in the familiar mining song "Keep Your Hand Upon the Dollar and Your Eye Upon the Scale").

Despite these changes, by 1902 there was little improvement in the lives of the miners and their families. Many miners and their families believed the PWA was corrupt and that its executive was controlled by the company and had little interest in the welfare of the men. By 1909 the miners had not had a pay raise in five years, yet the head of the PWA told a government representative that he would do anything to avoid a strike.

Also in 1909, the original head of the Dominion Coal Company, Henry Whitney, sold his interest in the company to foreign investors. So it was that miners disenchanted with the PWA, and faced with increasing poverty on one side and an ineffective union and absent, uncaring company on the other, sought representation from another union to negotiate better wages and conditions. They chose the U.S.-based United Mine Workers of America (UMW).

Miners loyal to the PWA, on the other hand, were keen to fight off the influence of a "foreign" union. The struggle was intense, and men who worked side by side became bitter enemies. The company singled out supporters of the UMW for the hardest, lowest-paying jobs and used company police to report on the attendance at organization meetings. Slowdowns, lockouts, intimidation, and threats continued into the winter to force the rebellious men who had voted for the UMW to give up the struggle.

During the miners' continuing efforts to gain fair working conditions in the first three decades of the twentieth century, they were often opposed, not only by the companies, but also by local newspapers, as in this editorial in the *Sydney Post* of May 14, 1909:

This lunacy is wrong in principle and against the wishes of the great majority of people whose only desire is to live in peace. They should be allowed to prosper in the bountiful arm of the company, living in company houses, fed from the company stores and steadily employed in the mines at good rates of pay.

Supporters of the UMW ultimately decided to go on strike in an effort to have their choice of union recognized. The company suspected that the success or failure of the strike would depend upon Dominion No. 2 in New Aberdeen, "the big producer," where a large number of men still supported the PWA. On the morning of July 9, 1909, the first day of the strike, hundreds of unarmed men, women, and children who supported the UMW gathered at the pit head to taunt PWA supporters arriving for work. Both G. H. Duggan, general manager of the Dominion Coal Company, and John Moffatt, secretary of the PWA, were mounted on horseback and led their "special constables" in an attack on the crowd. Witnesses reported that Duggan hit a woman in the face with a riding crop. Outraged, the crowd tried to pull Duggan from his horse (although an unsympathetic newspaper later reported this as an unprovoked attack on Duggan).

The company asked the town to call in the military to protect company property and was astounded when local civil authorities refused to endorse the request. Glace Bay mayor John Douglas pointed out that any vandalism was the fault of the company police as much as the strikers. J. B. McLachlan, leader of the pro-UMW movement, offered the services of out-of-work members of the UMW to protect the property, citing their interest in ensuring job sites were safe. Rebuffed by the town, the company approached the Cape Breton county council, which complied with the request for a military presence. Soon, five hundred troops and equipment were loaded onto a train in Halifax for the sixteen-hour trip to Glace Bay. Once they arrived, the troops, with machine guns and fixed bayonets, surrounded every pit head.

Most provincially and federally elected representatives failed the miners, as did the judiciary. The miners fared no better at the hands of many of their religious leaders. Sunday sermons often aimed hell-fire and brimstone at the striking miners. One of the most egregious examples of support for the company came when some three thousand UMW supporters marched from Glace Bay to Dominion. They crossed Cadegan's Brook, and rounding a turn, were met with machine guns set up on the Immaculate Conception Church steps with soldiers ready to fire on the marchers. The leaders of the march turned the parade around and led the men safely back to Glace Bay.

With the arrival of troops in 1909, the company police and soldiers began a reign of terror in Glace Bay and surrounding areas. Mass and brutal evictions from company houses ensued.

The UMW provided some support to the strikers' families, including food, shelter, clothing, and medical bills throughout the winter. Union leader J. B. McLachlan estimated the UMW's expenditure in Nova Scotia to be $1.5 million. The company employed numerous tactics against union leaders, including an injunction to desist "watching and besetting" coal company property. Strikebreakers were brought in from Europe, the rest of Canada and, surprisingly, from rural Cape Breton as well as from Newfoundland. In fairness, many imported workers were unaware that they would be employed as strikebreakers and refused to work under those conditions. Disunity among the men and deprivation eventually drove them back to work. Both the strike and the union failed.

Despite the significant profits the company made during World War I, by 1917 miners were left with little or no improvement in wages. In the end, the PWA and local UMW supporters finally joined forces to form the Amalgamated Mine Workers of Nova Scotia. The new union lasted only a short time and membership in the UMW soon revived.

Father John Fraser was born in Saint Andrew's in Antigonish County and studied at the Grand Seminary in Quebec where he probably met the future prime minister, Wilfrid Laurier. Before coming to Glace Bay, Father Fraser taught Latin Classics at St. Francis Xavier. From there he arrived at Saint John's Parish in Glace Bay in August 1908 in the middle of the town's labour struggles.

Within a year company police and soldiers were physically ejecting the families of UMW supporters from their homes. Father Fraser defied the company, media, politicians, and many other clergy by opening his church basement to these displaced families. He was openly criticized by the *Sydney Record* newspaper, which launched a public denunciation of his support for the striking miners.

Father Fraser stated his case in local papers and was quick to respond when unsympathetic newspapers misrepresented his support for the miners. He was outspoken in declaring that the company had precipitated the strike knowing the union did not have enough money to sustain miners on strike. Father Fraser also wrote a series of letters to Prime Minister Laurier explaining the situation in Glace Bay and asking for help. It is clear from these letters that Fraser and Prime Minister Laurier knew each other personally, yet the appeals fell on deaf ears.

In sermons, Father Fraser reminded his parishioners of the importance of maintaining the peace. He pointed out how public opinion at home and abroad was being poisoned by "misleading and slanderous reports sent out…by mischievous liars." He told his parishioners that the peaceful behaviour of the miners would result in public opinion slowly but surely turning in their favour. He spoke strongly and firmly against the company and against the PWA and reminded the men to stick together in their struggle.

Father Fraser remained at Saint John's Parish until 1916. He died at Saint Martha's Hospital in 1918.

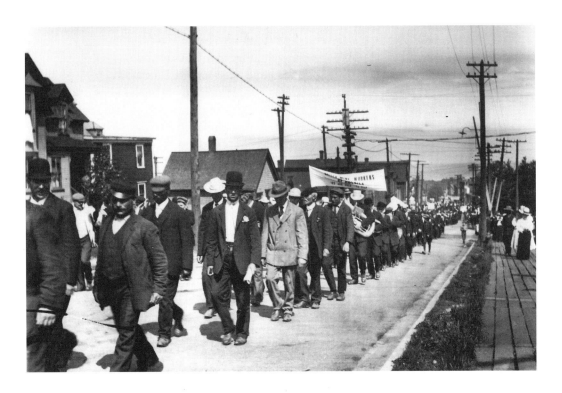

LABOUR DAY PARADE AT CHAPEL HILL, C.1912

These men are marching up Main Street in Glace Bay on Labour Day, 1912. Just three years earlier, many of these same men participated in the disastrous 1909 strike that saw families thrown into the streets and friend fighting friend for the right to have his union represent the miners.

Throughout the nineteenth and early twentieth centuries, miners faced a constant struggle for a living wage and decent working conditions, often while also being held hostage by their debts to company stores. Their leaders were called communists, malcontents, and rabble-rousers by a greedy corporation, hostile politicians, and newspapers. Through it all, miners never lost faith in the eventual victory of labour. To enforce the idea of the dignity of the worker, miners wore their best clothes and conducted their labour marches with decorum. The clothing may not have been expensive, or in the latest style, but it was clean and well-pressed, not an easy task in a town where a change in the wind could blacken a clothesline and where a wooden sidewalk in the downtown was all that protected shoes and hems from the muddy roads.

Troops arrive in Glace Bay by train, 1922

After a number of Montreal businessmen established the British Steel and Coal Company, better known as BESCO, to buy the Dominion Coal Company's assets in the Cape Breton coal fields, the company immediately set out to improve profits at the expense of the miners. The company cut wages in 1922, and the miners went on strike on August 14. Within hours of the strike being called, BESCO president Roy Wolvin appealed to the mayor of Glace Bay to request federal troops. As was the case in 1909, town council refused but the county agreed, and within hours troops were on the way from Halifax.

On August 16, the troop train from Halifax reached No. 2 colliery, where 250 soldiers unloaded machine guns, five eighteen-pound field guns, ammunition, and supplies. Guards were posted and the colliery soon became a military encampment:

> While on the way out to the mines, at one place about three hundred miners had gathered on the track and they remained there until it was evident that the engineer was not going to stop, then they jumped clear of the rails and delivered a fusillade of stones at the cars as they passed breaking several windows. No one was injured but the incident is evidence of the hostile attitude of the miners toward the introduction of troops into the district.
>
> (*Century in Review*)

More troops arrived from Quebec and Ontario by the end of the same week.

An agreement with local union leaders brokered by Nova Scotia

premier George Murray was reached on August 18 and presented to
BESCO president Wolvin in Montreal. Wolvin agreed to the terms.
The agreement called for the miners to take a cut in pay, but a smaller
one than was first proposed by the company and some substandard
wage rates were eliminated. The agreement was to run for sixteen
months. Troops were withdrawn and the miners officially approved
the agreement on August 31 and went back to work on September 4,
1922.

J. B. MCLACHLAN,
c.1930

J. B. McLachlan immigrated to Canada from Scotland with his family in 1902. In an industry that attracted young men, he was, at the age of thirty-three, already a senior miner in the coal fields. His union activities soon had him blacklisted from the mines, but he nevertheless became one of the preeminent labour leaders in the history of Cape Breton. McLachlan was one of the leaders who tried to have the United Mine Workers recognized by the company in the early 1900s, and his organizing efforts continued for most of his life.

On June 30, 1923, the federal government sent troops into Sydney to protect BESCO property against striking steel workers. The provincial police arrived on July 1. That evening, a number of police on horseback attacked pedestrians on Victoria Road in Whitney Pier causing extensive injuries to people and damage to property. The incident was reported to McLachlan, by that time a well-respected labour leader, in Glace Bay, and he wrote a letter to union members outlining the attack. UMW president Dan Livingstone delivered a copy of the letter to BESCO vice-president D. H. McDougall. On July 6, McLachlan and Livingstone were arrested and taken to Halifax overnight. Livingstone was eventually freed without charge, but McLachlan was charged with "publishing false news" (a specific charge under Section 136 of the Criminal Code) for the letter he wrote describing the attack, and also with seditious libel.

From the start, McLachlan faced an uphill battle. First, the trial was held in Halifax rather than in Cape Breton, where the offence was alleged to have taken place. Defence lawyers proved that the information in McLachlan's letter was correct, that it was not "published" but sent to a specific group of people, and that the eventual "publication" occurred when the BESCO vice-president gave a copy of the letter to a reporter demanding that it be published in a Halifax newspaper. While the evidence proved McLachlan was innocent of the charges, Judge Humphrey Mellish, a former coal company lawyer, nevertheless instructed the jury to find McLachlan guilty, claiming that what he had written fell within the definition of sedition because it was "calculated to cause unrest": "The issue is not whether the statements are true. There are many things that are true and cannot be published. It is not a question of the truth of the statement, but whether it was said with the intention of creating dissatisfaction and disturbance." McLachlan was sentenced to two years in the Dorchester penitentiary. A campaign for his release began almost immediately.

The sentence caused protests across the country and from numerous labour organizations in British Columbia, Alberta, Manitoba, Ontario, Quebec, and New Brunswick. Support for McLachlan intensified when his appeal, requesting his release or a new trial in Cape Breton, was denied. J. S. Woodsworth, a labour MP and later leader of the Cooperative Commonwealth Federation (CCF) Party, took up McLachlan's cause. Woodsworth himself had been charged with sedition at the time of the Winnipeg General Strike in 1919 but never brought to trial.

But not everyone opposed the sentence. Local member of Parliament George Kyte argued that McLachlan should remain in prison and BESCO president Wolvin called McLachlan, an admitted communist, a "dangerously clever Red," and blamed him for the unrest in the mining communities.

McLachlan was released from prison in March 1924, after intervention from the Department of Justice in Ottawa. His train stopped in New Glasgow, where he received a huge reception from Pictou County coal miners. After a speech there, he went on to a hero's welcome in Sydney. Finally, the tram that took him to Glace Bay was met by thousands of cheering supporters. As the police reports of the day attest, "He returned quite the conquering hero."

After arriving back in Glace Bay, McLachlan ran the union newspaper the *Maritime Labour Herald*, but a year later, during the 1925 strike, the paper's office suffered its fourth and worst fire. The building and its contents were completely destroyed. McLachlan determined that if the magazine offices were to avoid further damage, it would have to operate without him.

McLachlan's health had deteriorated during his incarceration in Halifax and Dorchester and became worse after his release. Although he remained quiet during the 1925 strike, his presence was felt. He warned immigrant workers to stay out of the lead in crowd actions lest they be blamed.

McLachlan had joined and promoted the Communist Party in the 1920s, even travelling to Russia to witness the revolution first-hand. But in 1936, McLachlan resigned from the party, deploring its "sad march to the right." He retired to his home in Steele's Hill where he died of tuberculosis in 1937. He remains an icon in Cape Breton labour history.

After police attacked civilians in Sydney, miners in Glace Bay threatened strike action in support of the steel workers if the provincial police were not withdrawn. The troops were not removed, and the miners voted to remain on strike until McLachlan and Livingstone were released. Promises of support came from the Alberta district of the UMW, but the head of the union, John L. Lewis, refused to recognize the validity of the strike and would not send funds. He revoked District 26's charter and instructed the company to divert the check-off to leaders he selected. The miners had to return to work, but soon those leaders were forced to declare a strike when the company posted another wage cut. The UMW leadership negotiated a contract that the men voted down. The company decided to implement it anyway.

**J. E. McClurg,
BESCO vice-
president, c.1920**

In 1925 the company planned further wage cuts. While an arbitration committee, stacked in favour of the company, was struck, the company planned for a strike. When reporters asked BESCO vice-president J. E. McClurg about the possible effects of a strike, he said the miners would be forced to return to work because the company held all the cards. McClurg claimed the miners wouldn't be able to survive the privation, and then spoke the infamous words that became a rallying cry for the strikers: "They can't stand the gaff."

The company was most anxious to subdue the rebellious union locals at New Aberdeen, Caledonia, and Donkin, so it made serious cuts to the days worked at these pits to force the miners' families into debt at the company stores. Then the stores were ordered to cut off credit in those areas. BESCO then closed mines in Reserve, New Waterford, Glace Bay, and Sydney Mines and cut off credit at all company stores. During most strikes, the union kept some men underground to maintain pumps and machinery to keep the mine ready for production. But with the company's increasingly harsh actions, District 26 called for 100 percent strike action. Only those manning the New Waterford power plant were exempt from the walkout.

While politicians, union members, and newspapers from other parts
of the country pleaded with the federal government to help the people
of Glace Bay, local politicians stood by their story that only a few malcontents were embarrassing the peaceful and happy people of the area.
This photo shows some of these supposed malcontents.

William Carroll and George Kyte, Liberal MPs from Cape Breton
South and Richmond, assured the House of Commons that life in
Glace Bay went on as usual and that most people were living well.

Those organizing and using relief programs disagreed. The efforts
of Group of Seven artist Lawren Harris and Rev. F. A. McAvoy, pastor
at the Glace Bay Baptist Church, resulted in the *Toronto Star* organizing support for the Glace Bay miners. Harris wrote a series of articles
sympathetic to the miners between January and June of 1925 while
McAvoy, in addition to organizing the relief effort in Glace Bay, met
with Parliamentary committees and gave interviews to the *Star* about
the difficult circumstances that existed in Glace Bay.

COMPANY STORE IN
RESERVE MINES AFTER
A STRIKE, 1925

When the miners declared a 100 percent strike, pulling all the men out of the mines, the coal company cut off power to the hospital in New Waterford. On the morning of June 11, 1925, angry miners in New Waterford, determined to restore electricity and water to their homes and families, marched on the Waterford Lake power plant where they were met by a wall of company police on horseback and brandishing guns. The police, firing their guns indiscriminately, charged into the crowd of miners. Many men were injured and one, William Davis, a thirty-seven-year-old father of ten, was fatally shot. The miners swarmed the power plant, overpowered the company police, and marched them off to the town jail. June 11 (Davis Day) has since been commemorated as a day when miners stop their work to remember Davis and all those who lost their lives underground.

For several nights after June 11, miners raided company stores to feed their families and then burned some stores to the ground. Most stores never reopened. The looting and burning of the company stores led to the return of federal troops. The government sent a bill for the army's services to the Glace Bay municipal government which, as in the past, refused to pay it. Poet and orator Dawn Fraser summed up the feelings of the mayor and council in his well-known poem "Send the Bill to BESCO."

In the summer of 1925 the provincial Liberals lost the election to the Tories. Former Glace Bay mayor Gordon Harrington was named provincial minister of mines. He struck a royal commission that recommended miners accept a wage cut in return for other concessions. The union supported the results of the commission. Harrington implemented the report's findings, but also took steps to improve working conditions in the mines throughout the province.

In March 1932, the company cut wages and shifts. UMW president D. W. Morrison urged miners to accept the cuts and stay on the job until the union convention in mid to late April. The company told the royal commission that it lost $1.8 million, while Morrison told the same commission the loss to the miners was three times that much. He claimed bad management and poor sales ability caused the company's losses.

While strife between the company and the men continued throughout the 1930s and 1940s, it would never again reach the same level of conflict as during the 1909 and 1925 strikes.

When Lawren Harris painted *Glace Bay Miners' Houses* and wrote articles for the *Toronto Star* in the winter and spring of 1925, many believed he overstated the poverty in Glace Bay. Charles Hill, curator of Canadian art at the National Gallery, described the bleakness of *Glace Bay Miners' Houses*: "Two rows of thin, starved, houses stand like sepulchres or crucifixes on the skyline." Harris's painting was exhibited in the aftermath of the most violent and protracted strike at the BESCO collieries in Glace Bay.

Harris's almost daily articles in the *Star* told readers about the misery inflicted on the people of Glace Bay by a cruel mining company. He praised and supported the work of Rev. Dr. F. A. McAvoy, a pastor at the Baptist Church who headed a relief commission composed of energetic and dedicated people from the town. Harris wrote that "only by the quickest thinking and most strenuous work could McAvoy and his committee keep one day ahead of starvation."

It is unclear whether Harris and McAvoy met in Glace Bay or whether Harris came to Glace Bay because he knew McAvoy. In any event, Harris spearheaded the *Star*'s focus on events in Glace Bay and a subsequent fundraising event by the newspaper and Toronto labour unions. The names of donors appeared daily in the *Star* until June 1925. The campaign must have been successful: Referring to one rally in support of Glace Bay miners, the newspaper apologized that due to bad weather only between two hundred and three hundred people showed up.

Rev. Dr. F. A. McAvoy, a tall man who had lost an arm in a farm accident, was pastor of the Baptist Church on York Street in Glace Bay in the early 1920s. Born in Ontario, he came to Glace Bay from a pastoral farming village in Nova Scotia's Annapolis Valley. Like Father Fraser some fifteen years before, McAvoy came face to face with extreme poverty inflicted on a town by a company bound to increase profits by cutting miners' earnings. (Wages had been cut in 1922 and 1923.) When the miners were faced with a 35 percent cut in pay in 1924, they threatened strike action.

In anticipation of a strike, the company instituted a pattern of sporadic shift cuts for months, and when families were near desperation, it closed the company stores in what it deemed "rebellious" areas. Realizing that near-destitute families would be driven to starvation, McAvoy led the formation of a relief committee, the Glace Bay Relief Association, and every merchant in town helped. On the first day nearly two hundred families were fed. The committee subsequently set up four stations in various parts of town. The town council donated five thousand dollars, and the UMW sent another four thousand. Meanwhile, McAvoy had already started a campaign for outside funds to help with relief efforts.

A 1925 photo of the Glace Bay Relief Association in the *Toronto Star* shows Rev. Dr. McAvoy; Mrs. John Casey; Rev. A. M. MacAdam; Mrs. E. McKay Forbes, wife of the former mayor of Glace Bay; Mrs. D. W. Morrison, wife of the (then) current mayor of Glace Bay; Mrs. Norman MacLeod; and Mrs. John T. MacPherson, one of the most prominent and beloved Salvation Army workers in Eastern Canada.

REV. DR. F. A. MCAVOY'S GRADUATION PHOTO, C.1919

McAvoy also met with House of Commons committees in Ottawa to ask for assistance for the Glace Bay miners and their families. McAvoy's message was continually contradicted by Nova Scotia's MPs, who insisted that the majority of citizens in Glace Bay were living in comfort, and that the plea for help was a result of a few "Reds" intent on promoting communism. From January to June of 1925, several articles on Glace Bay appeared in the *Star*, including an interview with McAvoy.

In the interview, McAvoy strongly disputed Lunenburg MP William Duff's fears that Parliament was being asked to sympathize with communists:

It is an utterly erroneous idea that the Cape Breton miners are reds. Our men are neither red nor radical, they are progressive. They do not look to stay in a rut. They are men who see the real things in life and are constructionists, not destructionists. They are as loyal to Canadian institutions as men in any other party of Canada. If that were not so, we would not have 4000 returned soldiers in our ranks. We're losing, however, the young men, our very finest blood, at a rate of 200 per week, mostly to the States. There is talk of 1,000 war veterans migrating en masse to the Argentine Republic. It is a tragedy that these men, many of whom have war wounds and war medals should be forced on pain of starvation to leave the land for which they fought and bled.

McAvoy and Harris were instrumental in the *Star*'s efforts to not only increase awareness of the Glace Bay labour issues, but also to fundraise in support of the miners. Headlines in the *Star* in 1925 read:

"Families of N.S. Miners Clothed In Old Sacks"
"Cannot Interfere Says Murdock" [federal minister of labour]
"Officials Will Man Pumps and Fans"
"Sees no chance of Peace in Cape Breton's coal area"
"Makes Dominion-Wide Plea to help Fellow Canadians"
"Many Now Starving in Glace Bay District"

In 1926, McAvoy left Glace Bay. A Glace Bay Baptist Church history records his fine singing voice that brought many to the church.

Gordon Sidney Harrington was born in Halifax where he earned his law degree at Dalhousie University in 1904. Soon after graduating, he settled in Glace Bay and married Catherine MacDonald. An able debater and a charismatic personality, Harrington won over the towns-people, and he was elected mayor in 1912 at the age of twenty-eight.

In 1915, Harrington resigned as mayor to enlist in the army. He worked as a recruiter, served in Europe, and in 1917 was promoted to the rank of colonel when he was appointed to the staff of the Overseas Ministry in London, where he served as assistant deputy min-ister and then deputy minister. At the end of the war Harrington returned to Cape Breton. He worked as a legal advisor to the UMW and defended J. B. McLachlan in his seditious libel trial.

Harrington ran for the provincial Conservative Party in 1925. Given the Liberal government's acquiescence to the coal com-pany's request for troops during that year's strike, it is not surprising that Harrington won easily. Named minister of public works and mines by new premier Edgar Rhodes, Harrington worked to improve rela-tions between the mining companies and employees in the province. He was largely responsible for improving conditions in the mines, and lobbied the federal government for a national coal policy.

In 1930 Harrington replaced Rhodes as Nova Scotia's premier. He was a popular choice, yet his hard work could not hold back the rav-ages of the Depression. Harrington's efforts to encourage idle miners to take over abandoned farms proved unsuccessful, but no one could question his decision to build a highway through northern Cape Breton that opened the land for Cape Breton Highlands National Park.

During the early days of the Depression, Harrington negotiated an agreement with the federal government and municipalities to divert funds previously given directly to individuals. Instead, he used it for make-work projects focused on building infrastructure, including improved roads and sewage systems. In Glace Bay, the coal company had refused to have its houses hooked up to the town's sewage system despite health reports that indicated that due to poor sanitation, the New Aberdeen area of Glace Bay ranked worst in Canada for child-hood death and disease. Harrington passed legislation to force the company to comply with the installation of water and sewer facilities.

Nevertheless, the ongoing economic downturn led to the Conservatives losing to the Liberals under Angus L. MacDonald in 1933. Harrington remained leader of the Opposition until his retire-ment in 1937. He died in 1943.

Clarie Gillis was born in Londonderry, Nova Scotia, and moved with his family to Glace Bay when he was ten. His family was evicted from company housing, and he recalled spending a winter in a church basement and later, in a tent. At thirteen years old, he went into the mines. Gillis's father worked in the U.S. during most of Clarie's young life and was blacklisted in the mines because of his union activities, but that did not deter young Clarie from becoming active in the UMW.

Elected as the first Cooperative Commonwealth Federation (CCF) MP east of Manitoba in 1940, Gillis brought to the House of Commons the refreshing, forthright, and sometimes blunt speech of a labour man. He spoke his mind even if it went against the party's views. His socialist leanings were practical, and he had little time for the more philosophical thinking of some of his party colleagues. Yet his words were always listened to with respect. He was the chief spokesman for the Maritimes, for veterans, and for a Canso Causeway. Prime Minister MacKenzie King had his staff notify him whenever Gillis was speaking and slipped into the gallery to hear the orator. Another member, an "arch capitalist," never missed a speech by Gillis, saying, "He preaches socialism, but he makes extremely good sense and it is a joy to listen to him." Former Conservative leader Robert Stanfield also praised Gillis: "His gift of expressing himself clearly and forcibly, his desire to fight for what he thought was right and his sense of fairness made him a national figure in the Commons."

During his years in Ottawa, Gillis argued for a productivity council, which was formed three years after he left. He was among the first to call for a national energy policy, for federal participation in vocational training, for federal pensions, and of course, for the causeway.

Having served as an MP from 1940 to 1957, Clarie Gillis died in December 1960. A front page article in the *Halifax Herald* on December 19 painted him as a stocky, outspoken Cape Bretoner who would rather have a beer in a tavern with working people than sip wine with cabinet ministers.

LAWREN HARRIS SKETCH OF GLACE BAY MINER'S WIFE, C.1925

In 1917, as part of the Amalgamated Mine Workers union's wage negotiations with the coal company, J. B. McLachlan launched a contest for miners' wives in the coal towns. Women were invited to write and explain how they would maintain a family of two adults and five children on a daily wage of $3.50. McLachlan had the responses printed in the Sydney labour newspaper, the *Canadian Labour Leader*.

In their responses, women concentrated on providing the basic needs of food, clothing, and shelter. Although rents were low, company houses were cold and in disrepair, and there could be no "luxuries" such as floor mats or wallpaper. Because loss of work due to illness or accident could lead to instant destitution, women had to invest in costly insurance policies. The family diet consisted of potatoes, flour, and rolled oats with little meat or fruit. Most budgets submitted for the contest omitted items as common as salt, molasses, clothing, and school supplies, to name a few. There was certainly little money for entertainment, newspapers, candy, or musical instruments. One woman concluded, "[My husband's] weekly income won't cover the food bill and house rent alone, let alone all the rest of life's necessities. There are two ways out of it. Eat less or earn more."

Some women kept boarders to try to supplement the meagre and inconsistent wages from the mines. During times of extended strikes, these women consistently made something out of nothing. Even when there was financial support from unions, it was minimal and insufficient to sustain a family. Medical officers of health consistently reported borderline starvation. The fact that more people did not die from the poverty and malnutrition was in many cases due to the efforts of the community's women.

According to the *Cape Breton Book of Days* these were the prices at a Dominion Coal Company store in 1922:

Sirloin steaks and roasts...................22 cents/lb.
Butter.....................................40 cents/lb.
Sugar.....................................8 cents/lb.
Best hard wheat flour in wood...........$9.50 bbl (per barrel)
Extra fancy molasses.....................75 cents/gallon
Salt beef.................................14 cents/lb.
Tea.......................................50 cents/lb.
Overalls..................................$1.50 pair
Pit boots.................................$2.75 pair

STRIKING MINERS, 1949

In this photo, men manning the picket lines are dressed in their Sunday best. In the nineteenth and early twentieth centuries, Glace Bay gained a reputation as a hotbed of labour unrest. Most people who moved to the community at the turn of the twentieth century sought only to improve their living conditions and those of their families. But from the beginning Glace Bay was under the yoke of foreign interests that had little concern for, or obligation to, the workers.

Although strikes and slowdowns early in the twentieth century often failed to result in the fulfillment of miners' demands, miners did make gradual progress in terms of safety, wages, and benefits, until the declining markets for coal led to the closure of many of the mines.

Chapter 4

Churches, Hospitals, and Schools

THE SECOND SAINT ANNE'S CHURCH, C.1935

CHURCHES

Anyone doubting the influence of religion on Glace Bay need only count the number of churches that existed in the town up to twenty years ago. Glace Bay has the distinction of having the first synagogue in Atlantic Canada and what might be the smallest Greek Orthodox church in the country. There were Presbyterian, Anglican, Baptist, Methodist, Pentecostal, Salvation Army, and several United churches. Most Catholic churches were located in the various mining districts, except for Saint Anne's, which has had two magnificent edifices that dominated the skyline of the town. The first, built in 1864, burned in 1917. The second, equally impressive, burned in 1982. Most Protestant churches were built in the downtown in an area surrounded by Marconi, Park, Catherine and Commercial streets.

The fact that Glace Bay could support so many churches was a tribute to the devotion of the population as well as to the check-off system. It is generally accepted that the churches' dependence on the check-off is the reason most clergy supported the company in its conflicts with miners. Some preached that union leaders were godless communists. Yet religion gave people the strength to endure, and in times of trouble, religious differences were put aside for the general good. After all, Glace Bay produced Father Andy Hogan, the only Catholic priest elected to the House of Commons, and Sister Peggy Butts, the only Catholic nun ever appointed to the Senate. And during those same hard times, while some clergy were urging people to bend to the will of the coal company, others were working night and day to comfort the afflicted.

FATHER RONALD MACDONALD, C.1915

When Rev. Father Ronald MacDonald came to Saint Anne's Church in Glace Bay in 1898, he and Father Charles MacDonald began a campaign to have miners contribute to a check-off for a hospital. He studied hospital administration in private hospitals in the United States, and he negotiated with the diocese to have the Sisters of Saint Martha provide housekeeping and food services. Father MacDonald worked with community leaders and went underground to discuss the need for a hospital with the miners. Within two years the hospital was built and equipped. When the hospital was opened in 1902, it was named for the patron saint of workers, Saint Joseph. It was owned by the miners, and it was completely paid for. Father MacDonald was made president of the hospital's board of directors.

HOSPITALS

Located on one of the highest points in Glace Bay, at the corner of
Main Street and Wallace's Road, Saint Joseph's Hospital and nurses'
residence could be seen for miles around. The sisters of Saint Martha
ran the hospital and nursing school and set high standards for care,
cleanliness, and decorum.

In the beginning, Saint Joseph's operated with two head nurses,
a surgical nurse and two student nurses, thirteen medical and surgical staff, and two consulting physicians from Halifax. From 1902 to
1915, Miss Janet Cameron—a graduate of the Massachusetts General
Hospital—was the superintendent, or matron, of the hospital and the
first to occupy the position. She set high standards for management
and nursing services. She resigned briefly in 1909 and was replaced by
a Miss Margaret Conroy, only to return in 1912 having completed a
course in hospital administration in an American hospital.

Saint Joseph's received its first accreditation in 1921. In 1939 a new
wing was built along Wallace's Road and the province built a tuberculosis annex. Following a survey by the American College of Physicians
in 1942, St. Joseph's was considered the most modern and up-to-date
hospital in Atlantic Canada.

Saint Joseph's served all of Glace Bay until the General Hospital
was built in 1914. At that point, miners had to choose which hospital
to support through the check-off, with the choice made largely on the
basis of religion—Catholics used Saint Joseph's and Protestants used
the General.

DR. WALTER LEONARD MACLEAN, 1908

Walter Leonard MacLean's father was a minister at the Methodist church in Glace Bay, but was transferred to Alberta, where Walter was born. The family eventually settled in Halifax, where Walter's father taught at Pine Hill Divinity College. Walter was a Gold Medal graduate from Dalhousie Medical School in 1908, and he was active in university sports. Following his residency at the Victoria General Hospital, he moved to Glace Bay. Walter joined the war effort in 1915, travelled overseas, and treated hundreds of wounded soldiers in his field hospital during the war. MacLean pioneered blood transfusions and even employed a rudimentary system for determining blood compatibility. He died during the war when his hospital was bombed.

Dr. R. A. H. McKeen, for whom McKeen Street is named, brought talented doctors, including Dr. Walter MacLean, Dr. K. A. McCuish, and Dr. Allister Calder, to Glace Bay before he retired in 1912. Like Dr. MacLean, Dr. McCuish also joined the army in 1915 and was later killed on the battlefield.

Dr. McCuish received his early education at the Halifax Academy and later attended Dalhousie University, where he graduated with a medical degree in 1903. He began practicing medicine in Glace Bay that same year as an assistant to Dr. McKeen, and later formed a partnership with Dr. Calder and Dr. MacLean.

Dr. Calder was born at Springville, Pictou County, on January 1, 1880. He graduated from Dalhousie Medical School in 1909, after which he took a post-graduate course in New York before beginning his practice in Glace Bay. Dr. Calder was attached to the medical corps of the 94th Regiment stationed at Glace Bay. Drs. Calder and MacLean were also medical officers in Glace Bay and wrote extensively, with Dr. M. T. Sullivan, about the suffering of the town's children, caused by poverty and chronic near-starvation.

Dr. Sullivan was born in Glace Bay on March 13, 1874, and graduated from medical school at McGill University in 1901. He was Glace Bay's first health officer, serving from 1901 until 1908 and again from 1925 to 1926.

Doctors hired by the coal company and paid through the check-off system had a secure income, but they had to be all things to all people—surgeons, trauma specialists, psychiatrists, marriage counsellors, and sometimes lawyers, and family friends. These doctors were always on call for thousands of miners and their families, and they delivered babies, performed surgery, and treated victims of mine accidents. Each year, one of these doctors was appointed a medical health officer, reporting to town council on the health of the community and making recommendations for improvement. Medical health officers were teachers, sanitary inspectors, and important social commentators and critics.

In 1908, Dr. Sullivan recommended medical inspections in schools. Three years later, Dr. W. L. MacLean made the same request, and in 1914, Dr. Green advocated medical inspections of schools and urged that children with tuberculosis be separated from healthy children. Nevertheless, medical inspections in schools were not implemented until after World War I when a school nurse was appointed. It wouldn't be until the 1930s that government would insist on improved sanitation to address the underlying causes of disease and poor health.

GLACE BAY GENERAL HOSPITAL, C.1940

When Glace Bay General Hospital opened, the staff consisted of three nurses, and its first superintendent was Miss Edith MacClaritey. During the hospital's first years, she cooked and prepared all meals for staff and patients, established business procedures, oversaw nursing, teaching, and engineering departments, and gave anaesthetics. She had general care of the hospital, ordering drugs and surgical supplies, and looking after the finances. Given the workload, it is not surprising that turnover was high among hospital superintendents: The General Hospital had seven between 1915 and 1943.

Student nurses provided free services. To be accepted for training, they had to be well-educated, healthy, and of good moral character. They received tiny incomes for their work and had to conform to strict dress regulations. They were not allowed to leave the grounds without permission and had to be in a state of constant readiness.

PICNIC AT THE GENERAL HOSPITAL, C.1915

In this photo, picnickers enjoy the day on the General Hospital grounds.

The check-off system guaranteed a certain number of free beds in both hospitals in case of a mine disaster. The system, however, did not guarantee sufficient staff at the hospitals. Lydia Adams's mother, Florence, a famous pianist and piano teacher in Glace Bay, was a nurse at the General Hospital before her marriage. On night shifts, she and one student nurse were responsible for the entire operation of the hospital, from the maternity ward to, if necessary, the operating room if emergencies, including mine accidents, occurred.

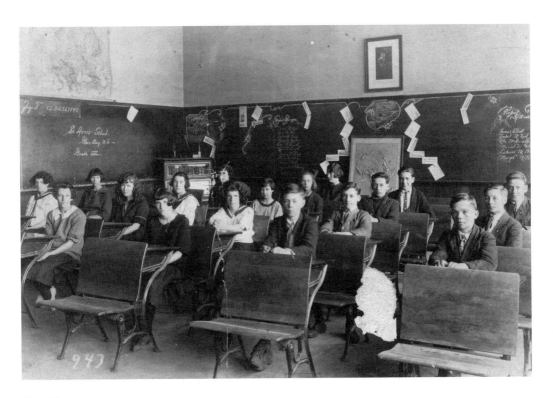

GLACE BAY SCHOOLCHILDREN, 1922

SCHOOLS

With the growth of the coal mines and the surrounding villages, schools were built in each community. At the Sterling, the original school was on Gordon Street, then moved to the Sterling Athletic Club until a primary to grade four school was built on Sterling Road in 1939. Unlike many other schools in Glace Bay, Sterling School had no religious affiliation.

The Sisters of Charity began running Saint Anne's School in 1864. Originally it offered high school for girls only. In 1922, Saint Anne's High School had more than one thousand students, the largest school population in Nova Scotia. Saint Anne's began admitting boys in the late 1920s. Prior to opening Saint Anne's High School to boys, all boys intent on high school education attended Glace Bay High. This school was on Brookside Street, but when Morrison High School opened in 1947, it was located across the street from Glace Bay High, which then became Morrison Junior High School. Morrison and Saint Anne's attracted students from Glace Bay as well as from the nearby towns Reserve Mines, Port Morien, and Donkin.

REBUILDING CENTRAL SCHOOL, C.1920

When Rev. Richard John Uniacke visited the growing village of Glace Bay in the late 1800s, he was intrigued by the rapid development he saw. Along with a new bridge (the Commercial Street Bridge), new harbour, new houses and churches, a new school—the first Central School—was under construction on Commercial Street. The second Central School on MacLean Street burned in 1919, sending students to church halls until the new Central School was completed the next year.

Chapter 5

Transportation and Communication

"PINKIE," C.1870

Glace Bay had the first locomotive on the south side of Sydney Harbour. Known locally as "Pinkie" (for unknown reasons), this engine was built in Edinburgh, Scotland, in 1867 for the Caledonia Coal Company. Pinkie hauled coal cars on the company line to a wharf on the south side of Glace Bay Harbour. The Glace Bay Mining Company also built a short railway to connect its Hub and

Sterling pits to a second wharf on the north side of the harbour.

The International Company at Bridgeport opened a rail line to the coal piers at Sydney in 1871. The same year, the narrow gauge Glasgow and Cape Breton rail line opened to connect its Sydney wharf with mines at Reserve and Schooner Pond. Shipping in the winter was difficult since both Sydney and Glace Bay harbours were often closed by ice, so the narrow gauge railway built a branch to the ice-free port at Louisbourg. These various lines became part of the Sydney and Louisbourg (S & L) Railway and were absorbed into H. M. Whitney's Dominion Coal Company when it was formed in 1893. It became the single railway in the Glace Bay–Sydney area as part of the process that saw Dominion Coal take over the area mines.

MACHINE SHOP AND TRAIN STATION, C.1910

The coal company machine shop on the left looks toward the railway station and Union Street. Bounded by Union and Reserve streets and Official Row, this was the main yard for the Sydney and Louisbourg Railway (the S & L). At the machine shop, tools were made, repaired, and even invented, for the mines and the railway. This photo is taken from the roundhouse area where locomotives were loaded on a track, hauled inside, and put into a stall that moved aside to allow another locomotive to be taken on board, forming a locomotive corral. It was here where the locomotives were stored and serviced.

Further down Union Street was the old train station. At one time passenger trains ran to Sydney and Louisbourg and often picked up miners heading to or from work in Glace Bay. The head office of the Dominion Coal Company and Glace Bay's first public library also once occupied space on Union Street. A 1921 fire destroyed many of the buildings on the other side of Union Street.

The Harbor, Glace Bay, N. S.

SCHOONERS IN GLACE BAY HARBOUR, C.1880

Glace Bay Harbour was dug out of what is now Renwick Brook in the mid-1800s because the original wharf at Port Caledonia (Big Glace Bay) kept silting in. By the start of the twentieth century, most of the community's supplies were being shipped in, and Glace Bay's main commercial area was at the intersection of North and Main streets. Prior to becoming the well-known stipendiary magistrate, A. B. McGillivray was shipping superintendent at the harbour. Near the centre of the photograph are the piers that loaded coal from Archbold mines.

Between 1862 and 1865 Rev. Richard John Uniacke travelled to Glace Bay twice on missionary trips. He wrote the following about bustling Glace Bay Harbour in his *Sketches of Cape Breton and Other Papers Related to Cape Breton*:

> About three years previous to my present visit, in traveling this road, I crossed over a small, marshy brook running into a little silent bay, upon a pole bridge about a hundred yards long...But now I found this little brook widened to a great extent. Twelve or thirteen large vessels, barques, brigs, and schooners occupied its basin as a secure dock or harbour, whilst they received their freight of superior coal, by a succession of cars, rolling along from the neighbouring pit.

With the rise of rail service, the transportation of goods through the harbour declined, but fishing continued. Many of the fishermen who plied the waters between Glace Bay and Newfoundland settled in Glace Bay. Many worked part of the year on the water and part of the year underground.

STERLING PIT CROSSING, 1902

Pictured above is Sterling Pit Crossing, the site of the former Sterling mine. The tram tracks under construction would cross the railway line going into what would become the Sterling yard. The mine operated at the intersection of McKeen Street and the Sterling Road. A four-family company house in the background stood at the intersection of the Sterling Road and Minto Street until it was replaced with Mike's Lunch. The houses on Minto Street were part of the Sterling mine complex and the manager's "Sterling House" still stands today.

Because Glace Bay grew from a collection of communities—New Aberdeen, Chapel Hill, Caledonia, Steele's Hill, Bridgeport, the Sterling—the advent of the tram car brought these communities together and helped develop the downtown. The tram also made for easier transportation to nearby Sydney.

TRAM CAR, 1902

In 1902, the Cape Breton Electric Company built thirty-four kilometres (twenty-one miles) of tram track in Glace Bay, including railway sidings, so trams traveling in opposite directions could pass. Italian inventor Guglielmo Marconi negotiated with the company to ensure the trams were at least a kilometre from the masts at his Table Head site to avoid interference with wireless transmission.

The trams ran every hour to Sydney and every half-hour throughout Glace Bay. The company also had a snow sweeper, a circular brush that revolved when the car was operating. During heavy snowfalls a snowplow was still required to clear the track in front of the tram.

In 1932, the U.S.-owned tram company went bankrupt, and the employees bought the assets, creating the Cape Breton Tramways Company. They expected the business to last a year or so, long enough for them to find other jobs. Instead it lasted fifteen. During World War II the owners could not buy rolling stock that was needed for maintenance and improved service.

As a means of transportation, trams gradually lost out to buses. Trucks moved freight, except in the spring when road conditions were poor. Eventually all roads were paved to make bus rides smoother. On May 15 1947, the era of trams ended officially. The last car carried veteran operators and administrators and was operated by long-time employees.

MARCONI TOWERS,
TABLE HEAD C.B.

MARCONI INSTALLATION AT TABLE HEAD, C.1902

On December 14, 1902, Guglielmo Marconi, an Italian inventor and entrepreneur, established sustained short-wave radio transmission between North America and Britain from the station at Table Head, foretelling an exciting new form of communication.

While the town was filling up with pitheads and people, houses and schools, churches and stores, few took notice of developments at Table Head, and it seems the manager of the Marconi property at Table Head took little notice of the rest of the town. R. N. Vyvyan, a native of Britain, installed the Marconi stations throughout Europe and America. At Table Head he expressed amazement at how men of different backgrounds and languages could work together to construct the facility. The co-operation and effort to build the masts were largely due to the leadership of Stanley Appleton of Glace Bay, who was hired as foreman.

STAFF AT THE MARCONI STATION, 1902

Marconi had intended to use Newfoundland as the westerly base for his transatlantic wireless experiment. He was dining in London with a Canadian postal employee when he was handed a letter charging him with violating the Anglo-American Telegraph Company's monopoly on telegraphic communications between Britain and Newfoundland. He decided to move his experiments to Cape Breton (some say at the invitation of Alexander Graham Bell), and "a party of dignitaries" met him at the wharf in North Sydney. Marconi was taken by train to Table Head, a site that delighted him.

Marconi obtained both moral and financial support from the federal government to set up on the east coast of Canada. He negotiated an agreement with Ottawa in which the federal government paid for construction of the station. In return, Marconi promised to provide transatlantic wireless service at less than half the cost charged by the cable companies.

While local people may not have paid attention to Marconi and his operations, a December 1902 edition of the *Sydney Post* noted that little progress was being made. But then, on December 14, the Table Head staff received news from the Poldhu Wireless Station in England that they were able to read Table Head signals for a sustained period of two hours. On hearing the news, the Table Head staff celebrated in the snow without coats or boots. Lizzie MacLean, who with her sister Mary Jane worked at Table Head, told her family that staff knew something great had happened when the usually reserved Marconi danced the staff around the kitchen that night. It was the first short-wave radio message to cross the Atlantic.

A misunderstanding between Marconi and the German Kaiser led to an unusual incident at Table Head in 1902. At the time, Germany was developing wireless communications as well. When a ship with the kaiser's son (and Marconi's wireless equipment) on board could not be accessed with the German system after it left New York, the kaiser accused Marconi of jamming communications. In retaliation, the kaiser sent a ship to commandeer the Table Head site.

In his book, *Marconi and Wireless* (1932), Vyvyan recounts that a German admiral and thirty officers came to the Table Head gates seeking admission. Vyvyan asked the visitors for written authorization from either Marconi or directors of the company. When none was produced, the Germans were refused admittance. The next day, about 150 German sailors gathered at the gate. Sensing danger, workers inside converged on the gate, and the Germans soon left for good.

The Table Head site attracted several dignitaries over the years, including Governor General Lord Minto, for whom Minto Street is named.

GLACE BAY POST OFFICE, C.1930

Glace Bay's first post office was built in 1838. It was located in Bridgeport and operated by P. Cadegan. In 1866 another post office was located on a street corner in Little Glace Bay. It was operated by William MacDonald, who was elected to Parliament and eventually appointed to the Senate. (The corner became known as "Senator's Corner" in his honour.) The post office pictured here stood for many years across from Carrol's drugstore on Main Street at Senator's Corner.

FIRST DAY FOR MAIL CARRIERS, 1928

It was more than sixty years after Glace Bay got its first post office that home delivery began. The youngest mail carrier was Gore O'Neill (second from left in photo), at just eighteen years old. To O'Neill's right is Ed Rogers, and to O'Neill's left are Charles Weeks, Roy Cameron, George Walker, John B. (Johnny Rory D.) McNeil, and Leslie McCorson.

GLACE BAY FLYING CLUB, 1935

In about 1930, the Glace Bay Flying Club bought a piece of land at Reserve and developed an airport. On June 29, 1935, the first airmail left the Glace Bay Flying Club for Halifax. On the plane that day were the pilot, Mr. Fowler; the mechanic, Mr. Power; district director of postal service, Mr. Fultz, and his son; and Sydney's assistant postmaster, Mr. MacKinnon.

In 1939 the airport became known as the Cape Breton Airport, then Reserve Airport, and finally it was called the Sydney Airport. Its name was then changed to the name that remains today.

MINERS' ANNUAL PICNIC AND TRAIN TO MIRA, c.1920

Each year during miners' vacations, coal cars would be cleaned out so children could ride in them to the site of the company picnic, while their parents rode free of charge in the passenger cars.

The trains were a familiar sight in Glace Bay from the 1890s through most of the twentieth century. Their initial purpose was to carry coal, but in 1894 the S & L (Sydney and Louisbourg) began a passenger service between Glace Bay, Sydney, and Louisbourg. It often picked up men on their way to work in the mines. In the early part of the twentieth century, special Saturday night trains brought people from Port Morien and other villages into Glace Bay to shop, meet friends, and take in entertainment. The S & L was a slow train, both because of the condition of the rails and because of the many stops it made. As a result, the line was nicknamed the "Slow and Lazy," and a Cape Breton song from the 1950s poked fun at the speed of the train by saying that passengers were able to lean out the window and pick blueberries.

Chapter 6

Commercial Development

GLACE BAY HARBOUR, C.1890

This 1890 photo of Glace Bay Harbour shows the coal piers that loaded coal from the Caledonia mine on the right. The piers for coal from the Sterling and Hub mines are in the distance on the left. The photo was taken before the arrival of rail service, at a time when most commerce was conducted through the harbour. Unfortunately commerce also brought illness. Sailors would pick up infections and carry them from port to port. In the distance on the right is the smallpox hospital that was located at McPherson's Point. Coal company houses stand between a corral at the bottom of Commercial Street and the harbour.

At this time, there was an expanse of land to the east of North Street that included a ball field and several homes. In fact, North and Lower Main streets were the business and social hub of the town (this would later shift to Commercial Street). There was a successful lobster factory at the wharf, and according to an ad in the *Glace Bay Gazette*, in 1904, Bigelow's on the corner of Main and North sold the finest quality canned goods, as well as Scott's Emulsion, a liquid vitamin.

The fishing industry formed a link between Glace Bay and many communities in Newfoundland. Many fishermen from Newfoundland settled in Glace Bay, bringing a distinctive Newfoundland influence to the community.

The area also housed those less reputable establishments that operate in all harbour towns. There were at least three legal drinking establishments and a dozen or so illegal ones. Brodie Avenue, which ran between Main and Commercial streets, was dubbed "Sneaky Street" because it was the route by which liquor was smuggled from the wharf to the various drinking establishments.

But on Sunday afternoons respectable people of Glace Bay would dress in their finery and walk up and down Main Street meeting neighbours and friends. A Mr. MacDonald owned stables on Lower Main Street. On Sunday, he decorated his horses and paraded them up and down the street.

THE PARK HOTEL, c.1896

In the area that would become Glace Bay's downtown, several hotels sprang up in the mid to late 1800s, including the Park Hotel. It became the home of the McCritchie family before it was turned into an apartment building, and it still stands at the corner of Park and Catherine streets. On nearby Bruce Street was the MacDonald rooming house and the more upscale King George Hotel. Both the King George and the original Glace Bay Hotel were destroyed in a 1921 fire that burned nearly all of Union Street, including the original Savoy Theatre.

SMITH'S HOTEL DINING ROOM, 1896

In the late 1800s, and before the amalgamation of the villages that created the town of Glace Bay, rapid expansion led to the construction of several hotels, some in the growing commercial district in the downtown core and at least three in the village of New Aberdeen: Smith's, the Sanderson, and Connor's. While the word "hotel" in some cases referred to a rooming house for transient workers, hotels like Smith's, with its white tablecloths, likely catered to a travelling society that included salesmen and businessmen with interests in the mining, fishing, and building industries.

The villages of New Aberdeen and Caledonia had commercial areas that operated in competition with the company stores. It is likely that salesmen supplying these businesses would have chosen to set up shop in nearby hotels.

Town Hall and McKeen Street, Glace Bay, C.B.

THE TOWN HALL AND MCKEEN STREET, c.1910

Commercial development on Main Street stopped at the railway tracks and then wound around McKeen Street. The Glace Bay Town Hall was built in 1901, and it housed government offices, council chambers, and the police and fire stations. Today it is a heritage museum. Along with the town hall, McKeen Street was home to several businesses.

Pete Lechysky made kitchen cabinets behind the town hall. The Alexandra, a huge, indoor rink with natural ice, stood at the bottom of Cottage Lane. A coal company supply yard and veterinary clinic were located at the site of the old Sterling mine, where McKeen Street met the Sterling Road. A field between the old mine site and the post office on Main Street was a gathering place for political rallies. To politicians and the press, this area was known as "Red Square."

When he visited the area in the mid-1800s, Rev. Richard John Uniacke
reported that a school was under construction on what became
Commercial Street. By the turn of the century, the school was surrounded by commercial establishments, including John R. Gillis
Jewellers, the Black Diamond Pharmacy, the British Canadian Co-op,
Rukasin's clothing store, MacIntyre's menswear, and Lighters' Jewellers.
Everyone in town could walk to Woolworth's, where a good cup of
tea and a piece of pie were always available at the lunch counter. The
Broadway Restaurant at the intersection of Main and Commercial fea-
tured a round neon sign, and in the 1950s the Salvation Army band
played in front of the restaurant on Sunday nights. The Grill, in the
Glace Bay Hotel across from the Savoy, and Vihos Sweets were other
well-known gathering places.

McArel's store, c.1910

McArel's department store on Commercial Street was billed as the largest such store east of Montreal, with three floors of merchandise, including everything from horse harnesses to groceries, and pickles and crackers in big barrels. The McArel family home and a three-storey warehouse stood next to the store near the bottom of Commercial Street. Just south of the McArel property was the Dreamland Theatre, one of several theatres in Glace Bay at the turn of the century. Next to the theatre stood Campbell's Hotel, managed by Dannie "Nonsense" MacDonald. The Mejduks later moved from Caledonia and bought McArel's store in the 1930s.

As the name implies, Glace Bay's Commercial Street featured many of the town's most popular merchants, including Phillip's ice cream parlour. Fried's was on the corner of Main and Commercial, along with Ein's millinery store. J. F. Merchant and Sons was located on Senator's Corner (at Union and Commercial streets) in a building that would later become the Health Dairy. W. S. Rice was on the corner as well as M. Lighter Jeweller and Optical. Max Marcus had a clothing store on Commercial Street and Cameron's building supply store was on North Street.

In 1918 Campbell's Drugs was on Senator's Corner along with Steven's shoe shop. Nicholson's on Commercial Street advertised coats on sale and Dr. Clara Tuttle's osteopathy practice was located over the People's Store. There were several bookstores in the area during the early part of the twentieth century, including MacNeill's on Senator's Corner; later Norman Lipschitz's store attracted serious readers. The last free-standing bookstore in Glace Bay was MacLeod's on Commercial Street.

Gus and Lucy Corsano ran the Health Dairy at Senator's Corner for thirty-two years. The Health Dairy held a profusion of fruits, vegetables, and other foods found nowhere else in town. It catered to the European community in Glace Bay and also introduced the palates of scores of residents to Italian meats and cheeses, pickled walnuts, and Gus's special pickles. Gus came to Glace Bay from Italy to work in the coal mines. Three years later he moved to Toronto. Lucy, too, had moved from Glace Bay to Toronto, where the two met and married in 1921. They moved back to Glace Bay in 1930, and opened the store in 1940.

At the other end of Commercial Street, Michael Minchorf operated a chip wagon. Originally from Bulgaria, he had lived in several places, including Montreal, before coming to Glace Bay in 1948. "When we [he and his wife] came here we were scared stiff because we thought the people were tough," he said. "We were told that the people here are always breaking windows. But when we had that chip wagon, they never once broke the glass. I have never seen people so friendly as those in Cape Breton."

MAIN STREET FROM THE ROOF OF KING'S THEATRE, 1928

With the arrival of the railway, commerce slowly began creeping further up Main and Commercial streets. Immigrants brought new businesses, such as kosher butchers and Chinese laundries; there were at least two kosher butcher shops in Glace Bay at the turn of the twentieth century and six or more Chinese laundries. Main Street also had shoemakers, iron foundries, barbershops, a newspaper, candy stores, a new post office, and several grocery and clothing stores. In a 1904 advertisement, Samuel's market on Main Street made it known it wanted to purchase fat cows and pigs.

DOMINION COAL COMPANY HEAD OFFICE, UNION STREET, c.1902

The first coal company office was built on Union Street in 1902, as was the railway station and the machine shop and foundry. By the turn of the twentieth century, Union Street featured at least one hotel, and several restaurants and retail businesses.

GLACE BAY TAVERN, 1920

Another thriving business of days gone by was bootlegging liquor. While it doesn't happen in Glace Bay anymore, in the early twentieth century the word was that those who weren't selling liquor in the town were drinking it. When Glace Bay was incorporated in 1901, 50 percent of the town's taxes came from temperance act fines.

The abandoned tunnels from old mine workings in the cliffs of the town provided great places for processing bootleg liquor. Kegs of rum were brought ashore in small boats and transferred to old mine tunnels where liquor was transferred from kegs to bottles. In at least one case, local youths were given a free bottle if they had helped with this task. Trusted locals were paid to help unload the kegs from boats.

In 1871 three legal drinking establishments were listed in Lovell's directory. Soon after, "Black Mick" Sullivan opened shop, followed by the most famous liquor peddler in town, Jack MacRea, whose tavern was nicknamed "Bucket of Blood" because of the many boxing matches that took place there. For the most part, MacRea and others were left alone as long as they didn't allow people to become too intoxicated.

There were at least sixteen illegal drinking establishments in the downtown at the time. Newspapers carried stories of fights that broke out, including one suggesting that it appeared someone would have to die before the area was cleaned up. Brody Avenue earned the name Sneak Street because illegal liquor that landed at the wharf could be delivered straight to the back doors of the drinking establishments.

There are rumours that in the past, some liquor was transported in milk bottles painted white to disguise their contents, and that some bootleggers (not in Glace Bay, of course!) dressed like priests in an effort to deflect attention as they went from house to house.

FISHING BOATS AT GLACE BAY MARINA, C.1930

For a time, Glace Bay was the heart of the lucrative swordfishing industry. Seventy-five to eighty percent of the swordfish landings in Canada took place in the waters off Glace Bay. Ray Goldman, who still runs the family fish business, remembers hundreds of fishing boats filling the harbour at the end of each day. The boats formed their own communities, with fishermen from Petit de Grat in one part of the harbour, those from Cheticamp in another, and those from the South Shore, Newfoundland, and northern Cape Breton in their own groups. The 1939 catch of 1,778,700 pounds was the largest the industry ever recorded. The average price that summer was ten cents per pound.

The swordfishing industry was ultimately shut down after the discovery of high mercury levels in the fish. Some Cape Breton fishermen complained that while Canadian boats were tied up, U.S. boats were getting premium prices for fish caught in the same waters off Glace Bay that were closed to Canadians. In any case, by the time the ban was lifted, the days when boats devoted to swordfishing filled Glace Bay Harbour and men with harpoons battled individual fish were over. By then, draggers caught swordfish along with other species.

For a long time, Newfoundland and Glace Bay fishermen shared a connection that was captured in a song written by Glace Bay's Lorn Johnson for a contest in the early 1950s. Lorn's paternal grandfather was a fisherman from Newfoundland, and one of the first to swordfish out of Glace Bay.

> We fish the Atlantic high and low
> While the miners work down under
> From the crack of dawn we carry on
> Through lightning storms and thunder
>
> Cape Breton's rule the coal mines deep
> But we're the seas commanders
> We fish today out of old Glace Bay
> And we're Cape Breton Newfoundlanders
>
> If you're in the Bay
> Hurry down I say
> Come aboard and take a gander
> I may be loud but I sure am proud
> We're Cape Breton Newfoundlanders.

The Sally Ann Bakery was one of several family-owned bakeries in
Glace Bay. The Sally Ann was named after owner Dan MacDonald's
wife. (MacDonald would become one of the town's longest-serving
mayors.) For a time, bread from the Sally Ann Bakery was distributed
by horse and wagon. In a town often divided along religious lines,
MacDonald, a Catholic, provided the horse that led the Protestant
Orangemen's Parade for several years.

Vihos Sweets was a favourite lunchtime, after-school, or after-skat-
ing gathering place for high school students. Students from Donkin
and Morien waited there for the bus that stopped around the corner
on Duncan Street, one of the few places where students from Morrison
and Saint Anne's high schools might meet. In the winter, after the
restaurant closed for the night, owners Chris and Mike Dezagiacomo
made chocolates that they sold across the province at Easter.

Just up the street from Vihos Sweets, young men sat on the fence
outside Saint Paul's. From there they watched the world go by, whether
it was young women they fancied or a friends in a new car. When
young men in town managed to buy or borrow a car, they headed to
Commercial Street to show it off to whoever was gathered along the
fence. Hunters also drove past the fence, making sure that whatever
they had killed on the hunt was seen by all who were gathered there.

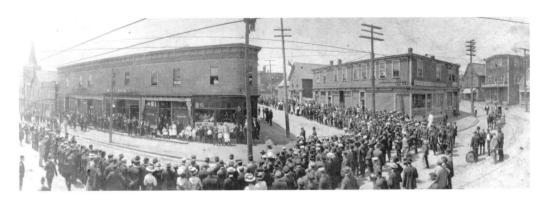

Senator's Corner was named for William MacDonald, former postmaster who became a member of Parliament and subsequently, a senator. In the photo above, a crowd has gathered to see a running race.

To the right is the MacRea block encircled Main, Commercial, and Union streets. The buildings on the right burned in a 1921 fire that began on Bruce Street. Among the buildings lost were three hotels, including the original Glace Bay Hotel, and the Savoy Theatre.

By 1927, a new Savoy Theatre had been built, and soon after, the Health Dairy began operating out of the Commercial Street building on the right.

Chapter 7

Sports

YOUNG LADIES' BASKETBALL TEAM, 1908

This image of a girls' basketball team was discovered in a box at the Town Hall Museum with no documentation. The photo tells a number of different stories: that of some delicate young ladies (who probably contradicted that image on the basketball court); the story of a photographer in a struggling industrial town projecting a romanticism on these young women; and it hints that in a town built on hard work for survival, there was still time for sports.

GLACE BAY FIRE DEPARTMENT ATHLETIC CLUB, C.1925

In 1925, the Glace Bay Fire Department was still located in the town hall and was then, as it is now, a volunteer operation. The department's athletic club, which organized track and field events, including high jumping and pole vaulting, consisted mainly of firefighters and young men the department hoped to recruit. Joey Mullins, who later competed in the 1960 Olympic Games, was one of the runners sponsored by the department. The athletic club also competed with other fire departments in firefighting skills, including hose-reeling races and ladder climbing. Later, the fire department supported ball and hockey teams.

In every community in Glace Bay, volunteers, mostly miners, built and managed athletic clubs, often with skating rinks on site. They organized and supervised dances and skating parties to raise money to buy sports equipment and to maintain buildings. They flooded rinks, bought sports equipment for their teams and for the young people in the community, and they taught team sports like baseball, hockey, rugby, and basketball. They did all this after working gruelling shifts in the mines. Community spirit and competition were strong within the town and with neighbouring towns.

JOEY BURCHELL, 1930

Glace Bay is well known for producing many great boxers who distinguished themselves in rings throughout the world. For the strong, talented young men of Glace Bay, boxing was a way out of the pits. Some found success in the short term, while others fared poorly under inadequate or callous management.

Mickey MacIntyre, "The Pride of Cape Breton," was originally from the Grand Mira area. He had a seven-year boxing career that took him across North America. At his peak he was the welterweight champion of Canada. During his last fight in Glace Bay in 1914, his opponent gave up and left the ring. Mickey died of pneumonia at the very young age of thirty-two.

As Mickey MacIntyre was ending his career in 1914, John MacIntyre's nearly twenty-year boxing career began. He boxed more than two hundred bouts in Canada, the United States, Paris, and London. He won both the Maritime lightweight and welterweight championships before retiring in 1932.

Stevie "Kid" MacDonald was one of seven brothers who were professional boxers. During his career, Stevie was junior lightweight champion of Canada, and in 1929, he was named junior lightweight champion of the world. He ended his career with a record of 181 wins and 6 losses.

In 1930, Glace Bay's Johnny Morris was the boxing instructor at Boston University and the Boston Athletic Association. He was also a state-approved boxing and hockey referee in Massachusetts. During World War I, Morris was the welterweight champion of the American Expeditionary Force.

Glace Bay produced other boxing greats: Joey Burchell won the Maritime featherweight championship at the age of sixteen; Glace Bay–born Eddie Provie was proclaimed the "Bronx Idol" by New York sports journalists on July 11, 1930; "Kid" Adshade was Maritime welterweight champion from 1946–1954 and scored the fastest knockout in Maritime history at the Glace Bay Forum.

And of course, there was Gussie MacLellan. Gussie MacLellan was born and brought up at New Aberdeen. He started his career by winning the Eastern Canadian featherweight title in 1946. He is well remembered for heavily promoting his own matches. Not surprisingly, he abandoned the ring to run a successful business as a boxing promoter.

CALEDONIA RUGBY TEAM, 1932

The Caledonia Athletic Club started in the early days of the community, although it was officially organized in 1927. When organized baseball started, Caledonia had stars like Johnnie McIntyre, James Knight, and Norman McIntyre. To play football, the boys often had to make a ball out of an old sock or an old baseball mitt filled with rags.

Caledonia had a regulation cricket pitch before the turn of the twentieth century, but the club was best known for its incredible rugby teams. The Caldedonia rugby club dominated the Maritimes' rugby scene for fifteen years through the 1930s and 1940s. The team won ten consecutive McCurdy Cups for supremacy in the Maritimes and won the McTier Cup—for Quebec-Maritime supremacy—on seventeen occasions from 1929 through 1946, losing only once, in 1932. Several players on those teams stood out, including Johnny Vey, who went on to become recreation director for the city of Fredericton, Clarence "Coot" MacLean, who died in Italy during World War II, and Sandy MacMullin, who died at a young age in an electrical accident.

Glace Bay had other athletic clubs too. The No. 11 Club was formed at the same time as at the No. 11 Colliery, but its predecessor, No. 3, had long been active in athletics. That club produced boxers Roddie MacDonald and Mickey MacIntyre, and later developed several talented football players.

TABLE HEAD ATHLETIC
CLUB MEMBERS,
C.1930

Dick Crowdis and Victor Farrell are credited for organizing the Table Head Athletic Club in 1929. In its first year of operation, the club built and paid for its clubhouse and the adjoining outdoor rink. That same year, the Table Head hockey team won the colliery league and the Burnstein trophy, and took the title again in 1930. The club was also instrumental in forming the colliery baseball league. It won the league championship in 1932 and placed second in 1933, losing to Springhill. The team won the Matheson Trophy in 1932 and 1933. In 1934 the juvenile team won the MacAulay Trophy and the ladies softball team won the Glace Bay championship. In 1935 the Club's original membership of twenty-five had grown to seventy.

The Hub Athletic Club was formed in 1922 "To promote clean sport and good fellowship among the citizens of the Hub." It won the colliery league baseball title in 1922, 1923, and 1924. The club was also active in hockey, running, and boxing. The original clubhouse was destroyed by fire and a new one that included an open-air rink was built in 1934. The club also worked to improve community welfare, hosting an annual Christmas dinner for children of the Hub.

The Sterling Athletic Club was formed in 1931 and quickly grew to seventy-five members. A campaign began soon after it was formed to raise money for "one of the finest structures owned by an organization of this kind in Eastern Nova Scotia." The club also constructed an adjoining open-air rink that became a great source of revenue for the club. (Ads in local newspapers listed bands that played during skating at the Sterling Rink.) In 1933 the club won the town's intermediate hockey championship and one year later, the intermediate baseball championship. It sponsored many amateur boxing championships and one of its youngest members, Joey Burchell, won the Maritime featherweight championship at the age of sixteen. The Sterling Club also carried out educational study groups and raised money for needy families during the hard years of the depression.

The Rockne Athletic Club, with Dan J. McDonald as president, was formed in 1934 for young men in Saint Anne's Parish. Within a year its membership grew to more than one hundred. Its football team ended the 1934 season in second place and in 1935, its basketball team won the Nova Scotia and Maritime titles. The club also sponsored plays performed by its members. It held monthly socials for members and friends, and its annual "At Home" open house held in the Saint Anne's gym was a true social event.

YMCA SENIOR
WOMEN'S NOVA
SCOTIA BASKETBALL
CHAMPIONS, 1936

Although the YMCA Athletic Club's primary role was to promote amateur athletics for young men, the YMCA had women's teams as well. It sponsored rugby, and its junior basketball team won two interprovincial championships in the early 1930s.

An open-air rink was built in 1933 and a YMCA men's hockey team entered the local league. The club had a room in the YMCA building, where there were facilities for pool, chess, checkers, and table tennis. The YMCA charged small membership fees and raised money through concerts and dances. The YMCA building on Commercial Street was later taken over by Knox United Church.

GLACE BAY AQUATIC CLUB HOCKEY TEAM, 1925

The Glace Bay Aquatic Club operated near Glace Bay Lake. In an effort to keep youth involved in sports year-round, it sponsored a women's hockey team that competed with teams in New Waterford and Sydney. In winter, the teams travelled by horse and wagon. Team captain Christine (MacDonald) MacIntyre (middle row on the right) recalled that her father used to walk from Glace Bay to attend games in New Waterford.

The Lakeview Sports Club was founded in 1933 by Alex McKay, Leslie Jobe, and Bill Cox to promote tennis and aquatics. The club's twelve original members built a double tennis court near Big Glace Bay Lake. The club sponsored swimming, diving, and canoeing competitions, and its members competed in, and won, many events in the area. In 1934, four members of the club—known as the "Cape North Four"—paddled from Glace Bay, around Cape Smokey, and almost to Cape North, establishing a record for long-distance ocean paddling in Cape Breton.

THE BLACK DIAMOND RACETRACK, C.1944

At the turn of the twentieth century, harness-racing events attracted as many as five thousand people to the Black Diamond Racetrack at the Hub. The track went into decline during World War I, but following the war, well-known horseman Matt MacAdam worked to restore the Black Diamond with the help of "Silent" Charlie Sweet and Billy Hood, famous trainers and riders. (Sweet was called "Silent" Charlie because he rarely complained about the outcome of races.) The Lewis and Hines families from Reserve were instrumental to the restoration as well. Pictured above is George Lewis with the horse Bonny K.

The annual May opening of the Black Diamond track was a gala social event in Glace Bay. In Cape Breton, it became common practice for several people to assist in the purchase and care of a horse; such horses became known as community horses.

Based at the Black Diamond, Sweet trained and rode several horses, including Glace Bay's community horse, Paleface. Competition among local community horses was intense, but under Sweet's direction Paleface was a consistent winner. During his career Sweet set more than twenty-eight course records. Sweet's expertise with horses led the provincial government to send him to the U.S. to buy breeding stock for the Agricultural College. Billy Hood established more than forty course records, many at the Black Diamond. Both Sweet and Hood were inducted into the Canadian Horse Racing Hall of Fame.

MISS RESERVE WITH LAMBERT TODD AT THE BLACK DIAMOND RACETRACK, 1929

Reserve's Lambert Todd was the first community horse in North America. Every week, girls from Reserve sold tickets for fifty–fifty draws that raised money to pay for feed and other expenses. These girls waited outside the mine, at the company store, and wherever people gathered. Because she sold the most tickets that year, Marjorie Hines (Walsh) received the honour of being named Miss Reserve Mines in 1929.

Once Paleface was purchased as Glace Bay's community horse, the owners wanted to show both Sydney and Reserve that Paleface was a horse to be reckoned with. An article in a Sydney newspaper reported that Paleface was paraded on downtown Sydney streets before being taken to Reserve, where the horse was at the head of a parade that marched through downtown Glace Bay.

A May 24, 1929, article shows how popular horse racing was in Glace Bay: "All attendance records at the new Aberdeen Trotting Park were broken yesterday when some 5,000 people crowded into the park to witness the first program of the racing season. The gate was almost as large as when Clarence DeMar, Johnnie Miles and other world famous marathoners raced here in connection with the 1927 horse racing program."

THE GLACE BAY MINERS' FORUM, 1939

In 1924, the Alexandra Rink on McKeen Street, a huge, closed-in natural ice rink, burned. Five years later, the fire department considered rebuilding, but the economic conditions caused by the Depression made that impossible. By then, the Glace Bay hockey league was playing its games in Sydney. In 1937–38 Glace Bay fans packed the Sydney Forum to see Glace Bay beat New Glasgow for the provincial hockey championship. Finally, a group formed to discuss how to build a modern rink with artificial ice. The group wound up selling shares with the understanding that no dividends would result. The effort started slowly, with about five thousand people paying ten dollars each for a share in the new forum. The town donated Cadegan's field for the building, and when construction began, it provided jobs for many local men.

The Glace Bay Miners' Forum opened on January 1, 1939, and from the beginning it attracted major entertainers. Forum manager Marty MacDonald was an inspired promoter and was able to attract important performers at the peak of their careers. In 1941 Gracie Fields played the forum, leading off a series of international artists, including Louis Armstrong, Benny Goodman, Art Mooney, Count Bassie, Duke Ellington, Guy Lombardo, Tommy Dorsey, and The Ink Spots. Country music performers included Hank Snow, Wilf Carter, Doc Williams, Webb Pierce, Red Sovince, Hank Williams Jr., Johnny Cash, and Farron Young. Also appearing were Gene Autry and his rodeo show, the Royal Lipizzaner Stallions, and Barbara Ann Scott, who had just captured an Olympic gold medal. There were sporting events, too, including major boxing cards and the Harlem Globetrotters.

And of course, there was everyone's passion: hockey. Cape Breton took hockey seriously, even threatening action if there was any hint of unfairness. The forum also hosted public skating sessions. Nearly everyone in Glace Bay skated. Valerie Kinslow, director of voice at McGill University, said that when she was growing up in Glace Bay, "You skated and you did music." And of course, the forum's skating sessions were popular for other reasons too: Many romances began with a brave young man taking a girl's arm while skating to the Donkin Band or vinyl records.

JOEY MULLINS, 1956

Joey Mullins, one of Glace Bay's few track stars, set many middle distance records. He established a world indoor record for six hundred yards in 1956, and ran in the 1958 British Empire Games and 1960 Olympics. He attended Nebraska State University on scholarship, and in 1960 was named the university's outstanding athlete.

**ALEXANDRA RINK,
1920**

When people in Glace Bay were not working, at home, in church, or watching plays or sports, it is likely they were skating. In the early part of the twentieth century, skating rinks were everywhere in the town. Most athletic clubs had skating rinks. The Alexandra Rink on McKeen Street was an indoor rink with natural ice. There were also outdoor rinks between Main and Commercial streets, on York Street, South Street, upper King Edward Street, and Brookside. Skaters could also skate on the marsh on Reserve Street, the dam on Beacon Street, and on many ponds and bogs, and sometimes even the harbour when it froze.

Hockey drew the largest crowds in Glace Bay, and people took the competition seriously, whether it was Table Head against the Sterling or Sydney against Glace Bay. Among the athletes honoured at the Nova Scotia Sport Hall of Fame are several hockey players from Glace Bay. Hugh MacKinnon was one of the best forwards in Canada from 1915 to 1929. Mickey Roach played with the Hamilton Tigers and led his team to the Allan Cup in 1919. He played 207 professional games in New York, tallying 75 goals and 27 assists.

John Myketyn was one of the best hockey (and baseball) players ever produced in the province. Born in Glace Bay, Myketyn played hockey for St. Francis Xavier University, helping the team win four straight university championships in the 1940s. He later played with the Sydney Millionaires and helped that team win Nova Scotia and Maritime championships.

THE GLACE BAY MINERS, 1955

Two playoff hockey series, several years apart, are still talked about in Glace Bay.

In 1941, Cape Breton's hockey league had teams in Glace Bay, Sydney, and North Sydney. North Sydney was the first to lose out, leaving Glace Bay and Sydney to fight for the title. Some digging by a Sydney supporter found that the Glace Bay goalie had failed to register and was therefore ineligible to play. The backup goalie was new and untried. So, the team sent him on a paid vacation and applied to the Maritime Amateur Hockey Association (MAHA) to use North Sydney's goalie, "Legs" Fraser, in his place. The Sydney team agreed with the arrangement, at least until Glace Bay beat them in the first two games. Sydney complained to the MAHA, which upheld the complaint. Fraser was out and "Leaky" Boates, the backup, was forced to play. Glace Bay lost the series. There was such an uproar that some Glace Bay retailers boycotted Sydney wholesalers, and some miners threatened to go on strike.

The second memorable series took place at the end of the 1955–56 season. In the three-team league, Glace Bay was in last place heading to the semi-finals. But the team surprised North Sydney by winning the series; it then faced Sydney in a best-of-five final series. The series went to overtime of the fifth game. Glace Bay won the game and went on to defeat Halifax for the Maritime championship. The team was forever known as the "Cinderella Miners."

Chapter 8

Arts and Entertainment

GAELIC CONCERT AT DREAMLAND THEATRE, C.1900

While the miners and their families struggled during the early days of the Glace Bay coal industry, they found joy in sports and entertainment. Poetry, music, and theatre were vital to the survival of the community.

Early in the twentieth century the town had, at the very least, six theatres and movie houses. From very early on, international stars included Glace Bay on their touring itineraries, and the town's stages proved more than adequate. Local talent was well appreciated by the town's residents, and many young people were encouraged to sing or play instruments. Almost every Scottish family had a fiddle, and the town hosted the first non-military pipe band in Atlantic Canada. Gaelic culture also flourished, through piping contests and Gaelic plays and concerts, such as the one in this photograph.

Writers, artists, singers, actors, and musicians were all part of the fabric of the town. Their imagination and talent inspired generations of artists, who either honed their craft on Cape Breton Island or enlivened the cultures of other provinces and countries.

PRINCE ALBERT BAND, 1902

Back row: Kenny Morrison (bass drum), Harry Roper, Malcolm MacDonald, "Red" Norman MacDonald, Rannie "Greedy Sandy" Macdonald, Hughie MacDonald, Donald Weir (side drum). Middle row: James Mosley, Rod "Noddie" Morrison, Norman Nicholson, Hugh MacVicar, Allan "Big Archie" MacDonald. Front row: Jimmie "Taylor" MacDonald, Arthur MacKenzie, band master R. W. Carmichael, Dan Willie Ferguson.

Much has been written about the poverty in Glace Bay in the early part of the twentieth century, but little attention has been focused on the culture that thrived in the town. The people of Glace Bay supported several bookstores; residents read and wrote prose and poetry. A number of theatres in town sponsored local stage productions and music concerts. Glace Bay's theatres were also on the "circuit" for international entertainers. In many families, at least one person played a musical instrument and many joined local orchestras. Bands were in high demand, from the MacIntyre Pipe Band that played for Celtic concerts and events, to the Prince Albert Band (pictured here), the AOL, and others that performed concerts and played at dances and skating parties. The tradition of skating to live bands lasted well into the middle of the century when the Donkin Band played for skaters at the Glace Bay Miners' Forum.

Orchestras also played at dances. Even during the Depression of the 1930s, people managed to find money to attend dances where their favourite bands were performing. Later in the century the music of Gib Whitney, Emelio Pace, and other live orchestras provided the music for another generation of dancers.

Born in Neil's Harbour, Lillian Crewe Walsh (1883–1967) was a prolific poet. She said she wrote what she knew, and some of her poems, like the "Ghost of Bras d'Or" and "Kelly's Mountain," went on to became popular folk songs. Mrs. Walsh was an early survivor of breast cancer and as a result, had to move her left arm with her right, yet her nephew Don Beaton remembers her as a charming woman with a positive outlook.

She settled in Glace Bay, where she ran a small store and wrote poetry, including "The Lady of the Loom." (She once said it was the sunlight glinting off a coal skuttle that inspired "The Lady of the Loom.")

> A lady sat beside her loom,
> With yarns of every hue;
> To weave Cape Breton tartan
> She only chose a few.
> Black for the wealth of our coal mines
> Grey for our Cape Breton steel
> Green for out lofty mountains
> Our valley and our fields
>
> Gold for the golden sunsets
> Shining bright on the lakes
> Of Bras d'Or
> To show us God's hand has lingered
> To bless Cape Breton shores

She took the poem to her friend, Elizabeth Belle Grant, who wove a sample of a tartan inspired by the poem. She picked yarn colours that featured prominently in the poem, and showed the sample to Mrs. Walsh, who thought it was perfect. It was 1957, and with that, the Cape Breton tartan was born.

Mrs. Grant immediately registered the tartan to guard against variation in its reproduction. As well, she handled all the business arrangements concerning the manufacture and sale of Cape Breton tartan material and products. It soon became impossible to keep up with demand, and the tartan had to be manufactured commercially. The women told reporters in 1958 that the success of the tartan was probably due to the muted colours, which appealed to both men and women.

Lillian Crewe Walsh also excelled at rug hooking. One rug depicting the British entering Louisbourg Harbour won first prize in a province-wide contest in which there were more than one hundred competitors. The rug hangs in the Glace Bay Library.

Elizabeth Grant is also remembered fondly by those who recall the Meadow Sweet ice cream plant on Alexander Street. Many residents remember Mrs. Grant selling huge scoops in double flat-bottomed cones. (Extra large scoops went to local children.) Tubs of the ice cream were easily recognizable by the pictures of movie stars that appeared on the inside of the lids.

One of Canada's greatest authors, Hugh MacLennan was born in Glace Bay in 1907. He attended Dalhousie University and Oxford University as a Rhodes Scholar. When he returned to Canada, he taught Latin and history at Montreal's Lower Canadian College. He taught English at McGill University until he retired in 1979.

While MacLennan lived only part of his life in Glace Bay, his novel *Each Man's Son* illuminates life in the town in the early 1900s from the perspective of a coal company doctor. *Barometer Rising*, MacLennan's novel about the Halifax Explosion, won him international recognition when it was published in 1941. But he was best known for *Two Solitudes*, a novel about the English-French divide in Canada. MacLennan won four Governor General's Awards for Literature. He died in 1990.

In 1919, Marguerite MacDougall became the first person to graduate from Mount Saint Vincent College with a degree in music. She brought her talent back to Glace Bay, where she influenced generations of musicians. Whether developing the scores for silent movies at the Savoy, working with local students in festivals, playing for stage productions, or accompanying international stars, Marguerite performed with charm and grace. It was well known that if a child performing in a festival started in the wrong key, Marguerite would immediately change the accompaniment to that key.

Many of her students have gone on to national and international acclaim. Lydia Adams is the conductor of Canada's Amadeus Choir and the Elmer Iseler singers. Lydia and Stuart Calvert sang in the choir at the wedding of the Prince of Wales and Lady Diana Spencer. Calvert is now a conductor in London. Valerie Kinslow is dean of voice at McGill University and performs medieval music with Tafelmuzic. Lorna MacDonald is the Lois Marshall Chair of Voice at the University of Toronto. The late opera singer Annon Lee Silver was a student of Marguerite's, as was Debbie Jeans of Sydney, who Marguerite's daughters claim became like another sister. Jim Petrie of the Halifax Feast Dinner Theatre was also one of Marguerite's students.

Marguerite MacDougall accompanied myriad musicians and singers who visited Cape Breton. She taught and accompanied jazz saxophonist Don Palmer, and she played for Barbara Ann Scott when Scott performed at the Miners' Forum following her gold medal win at the Oslo Olympics. Marguerite was even asked to play for Lassie when the dog appeared in Sydney. (She accepted.) She worked with almost every church choir in Glace Bay and played for numerous radio and television productions.

Marguerite would not have been able to accomplish all she did without the co-operation and help of her husband, Alex; he took an active role in raising their seven children and keeping the household going while holding a full-time job and, for a time, sitting on town council. Marguerite died in November 2007 at the age of ninety-nine.

KNOX CHURCH CHRISTMAS CONCERT, 1948

Many of Glace Bay's talented musicians started out in church choirs and performed at Christmas concerts like the Knox Street concert pictured here. If singers were interested in pursuing their talents in Glace Bay, it is likely they developed their skills in lessons with teachers like Marguerite McDougall, Harry D. MacNeil, and Florence (Travis) Adams. These dedicated teachers encouraged their students to participate in music festivals and concerts. Along with teaching their own students, they helped out with church choirs—Marguerite McDougall with high school choirs, "Harry D." with the men's choir at Saint Anne's, and Florence Adams with the choir at Saint Paul's.

Florence Travis grew up in a home where music was important both economically and for enjoyment. Her father and his brothers ran Travis Brothers Pianos and Organs on Commercial Street before losing the business during the Depression. Even during those hard times, young people would gather at the Travis household every Sunday night for a singalong. In fact, the singalong was where Florence met her future husband, Robert "Bob" Adams.

Caring for others was also important to the Travis family. Florence's father had a magnificent garden where he grew much more than their family needed, so he was able to provide many other Glace Bay families with fresh food to put on their tables. It was probably this emphasis on caring that led Florence to a career in nursing. While working as night nursing superintendent at the Glace Bay General Hospital, she studied piano and organ in Glace Bay and Sydney. She earned her music teaching diploma from Trinity College of Music in London, England, sending and receiving her papers by ship during the war. She and Bob Adams married in secret in 1944 because she would have lost her nursing job if she had married openly. When her marriage was finally discovered, she did lose her job and began teaching piano.

Bob Adams worked at the Forge (Central Shops) in Glace Bay, eventually becoming the foreman. In the early 1940s, Bob took night courses in drafting and other skills so that he could build a house for his family. Every day after work, he would bicycle over to the lot he and Florence had bought on South Street, building bit by bit the home where they would live for many years. While Florence was an active piano teacher, Bob was an integral part of the teaching team, driving children to and from lessons and feeding everyone who came through the door.

Florence taught piano to generations of children. She also conducted many children's choirs at the churches where she worked, most notably at St. Paul's Presbyterian, where her junior and senior choirs flourished. She also founded and conducted the Glace Bay Teenaires, a group of exceptional young singers who represented the town on tours to Kitchener, Montreal, and Scotland. Florence's own daughter, Lydia, is conductor of the Amadeus Choir and the Elmer Iseler Singers.

Both Florence and Marguerite MacDougall were social activists— they helped save Glace Bay's beach, raised funds for a new piano at the Savoy Theatre, and believed in bringing beauty and optimism to the lives of the town's students.

Several generations of young musicians were given their start in Glace Bay under the caring instruction of Harry D. McNeil. "Professor McNeil," as many of his students referred to him, taught from his spacious home on Main Street, a convenient location for both his students and for him, as he was also organist in Saint Anne's Roman Catholic Church.

Nowhere was Harry McNeil's influence felt more strongly or remembered with more gratitude than in the MacDonald home in Port Morien where organist David MacDonald (1952–2003) and his sister, soprano Lorna MacDonald, were raised. David's career as a concert organist and church musician took him to the great cathedrals and churches of Europe (Paris, London, Oxford, Munich, Strasbourg, and Rotterdam, among others) where his playing was internationally acclaimed.

After their regular Friday night piano lesson, Harry D. would often take David and his father across the street to the organ loft in old Saint Anne's Church. There Mr. McNeil demonstrated the organ and its myriad pipes and stops to David. At Dalhousie University, David cast aside thoughts of political science and ventured into the music education degree, majoring in the organ. Further study took him to McGill University and Paris. Within a few years, David MacDonald was among Canada's finest organists. He was recorded regularly by the CBC and released seven CDs of solo organ and choral music. His performances of the complete organ works of J. S. Bach were testimony to his life's devotion, and to his excellence as a great interpreter of Bach's music. Without the opportunity and encouragement provided by Harry D. McNeil, one of Canada's finest musical careers might never have begun.

THE SAVOY THEATRE, c.1935

The Savoy Theatre is a familiar Glace Bay landmark for all Cape Bretoners; the original burned in a fire in 1921 and was replaced in 1927 with the one that still stands today. An expansion in recent years has changed the appearance, but not the history, of the Savoy. The Savoy attracted a range of entertainers from boxers to traveling comedy shows, and it was also a venue for local talent, including music and elocution festivals, graduation ceremonies, concerts, and plays. It was also a cinema, and generations of children lined up on Saturday afternoons to see the cowboy movies and other features that came to town.

In this photo, the Savoy is on the right and the "new" Glace Bay Hotel is on the left. The old post office on Main Street is visible in the background (centre) of the photo.

THE KING'S THEATRE, 1928

The King's Theatre was a three-storey building on the Saint Anne's School property at the corner of Main Street and Official Row. Built in 1909, the King's sat one thousand people, and it attracted major international entertainers as well as local talent. The McIntosh Brothers, Bernie and Tony, staged musical concerts there. The King's had a gym in the basement and also showed silent movies.

Father Ronald MacDonald was well known in Glace Bay for his efforts in establishing Saint Joseph's Hospital. What is not well known is that during his time at Saint Anne's Parish, Father MacDonald was instrumental in the construction of the King's Theatre and the Alexandra Rink. The foundation of the theatre remained on Saint Anne's School property long after the building was moved, likely to New Waterford, where it was renamed the Strand.

The Dreamland Theatre, located near the bottom of Commercial Street just south of McArel's store, was a huge theatre where, at the turn of the twentieth century, English and Gaelic concerts took place. In this photograph, the Dreamland Theatre is visible on the left.

The original Russell Theatre burned early in the 1900s, and before it was rebuilt near the Commercial Street bridge, the Capitol opened at Senator's Corner where Joe Smith's clothing store stood a generation later. Any attempt to compile a list of Glace Bay theatres and entertainment venues will inevitably miss some, but over the years, Glace Bay residents supported a number of theatres, including those mentioned above as well as the Star, the Casino, the Jubilee, the Victory, and the Olympic.

Parade day, 1926   Even during the worst political and economic strife in Glace Bay, people found ways to celebrate, and parades were an important part of fostering town pride. Local merchants built elaborate floats and citizens lined the sidewalks to hear bands play and watch soldiers, firefighters, and police officers march through the downtown.

Even in 1926, the year of the most tragic and protracted strike in the town's history, a year when poverty and starvation threatened many, the town of Glace Bay still held a parade to draw people together.

NATHAN COHEN AND CHARLIE (A. D.) MCNEILL AT THE *GLACE BAY GAZETTE*, 1942

Nathan Cohen (1923–1971), a major figure on the Canadian arts scene and a feared and revered critic, was born in Whitney Pier, and at age nineteen, he became the sole reporting staff for the UMW-owned *Glace Bay Gazette*. Considering his university years, it is not surprising that he gravitated to the union-owned paper.

Cohen entered Mount Allison University in 1939 at age sixteen, but rarely went to class. Instead, he spent his time at the library, acting in theatre productions, editing university publications, and running the school yearbook. He attacked incompetent professors, challenged conscription, and questioned the war in Europe.

While at the *Gazette*, Cohen became a fierce critic of the poor conditions in the mines. Cohen eventually left the paper in 1945, two years before its demise, and went to work for the Communist Party's *Canadian Tribune*.

Cohen is best known as an uncompromising theatre critic and the host of CBC-TV's *Fighting Words*, a weekly discussion program. He was later hired by the *Toronto Star* as an entertainment columnist and then entertainment editor.

Cohen died three weeks short of his forty-eighth birthday in 1971.

Selected Bibliography

BOOKS

Ackerman, Jeremy. *Black Around the Eyes*. Toronto: McClelland and Stewart, 1981.

Currie, Sheldon. *The Company Store*. Ottawa: Oberon Press, 1988.

Dunn, Charles. *Highland Settler*. Toronto: University of Toronto Press, 1953.

Frank, David. *J. B. McLachlan: A Biography*. Toronto: James Lorimer, 1999.

Hornsby, Stephen. *19th Century Cape Breton*. Montreal: McGill-Queen's University Press, 1992.

Latremouille, Joann. *Pride of Home: The Working Class Housing Tradition in Nova Scotia 1749–1949*. Hantsport, NS: Lancelot Press, 1986.

MacAdam, Pat. *Big Cy and Other Characters*. Sydney, NS: Cape Breton University Press, 2006.

MacLennan, Hugh. *Each Man's Son*. Toronto: MacMillan, 1951.

McEwan, Paul. *Miners and Steelworkers: Labour in Cape Breton*. Toronto: A. M. Hakkert, 1976.

Mellor, John. *The Company Store: J. B. McLachlan and the Cape Breton Coal Miners 1900–1925*. Halifax: Formac, 1984.

Morgan, Robert. *Early Cape Breton*. Sydney, NS: Breton Books, 2000.

Newton, Pamela. *Cape Breton Book of Days*. Sydney, NS: UCCB Press, 1984.

Uniacke, Rev. Richard John. *Sketches of Cape Breton*. Ed. Bruce Ferguson. Nova Scotia Public Archives, 1958.

PERIODICALS

Cape Breton/Atlantic Mirrors, Glace Bay, various.

The Courier. Glace Bay, various.

Toronto Star, January to June 1925, various.

The Gazette. Glace Bay, 1920s and 1930s, various.

The Cape Breton Post. "Century in Review." December 1999.

Image Sources

Howard MacKinnon: i, 19, 48, 74, 91, 100, 117, 120, 121, 125, 128
A. F. Church & Co.: 1
Cape Breton Miner's Museum: 3, 9, 14, 27, 34, 38, 45, 49, 50, 51, 52, 56, 73, 86, 105, 110, 113, 119
Wayne Howie: 7
Maureen McNeil: 11, 30
Ken Walsh: 12, 53, 54, 115, 116, 136
Shirley Chernin: 13
Amelia Burta Valley: 15
Gloria Farmicoulous: 16
Glace Bay Heritage Museum: 17, 67, 75, 87, 107
Sue Edwards: 21
Judy MacLeod: 23
Dale Redmond: 24
Nova Scotia Archives and Records Management: 25, 37, 61
Glace Bay Historical Society: 31
Charmaigne & Eileen Curry: 41
St. Francis Xavier Archives: 47
Stewart Sheppard: 59, 63
Acadia University Archives: 60
Diocese of Antigonish: 69
Dalhousie Medical School Archives: 71
Herb Macdonald: 77
Sydney & Louisbourg Railway Museum: 79
Dominion Heritage Museum: 82
Evelyn McDonald: 83, 84
Inglis MacAulay: 88, 93, 94
Raymond Goldman: 91
Georgie Matheson-MacDonald c/o Glace Bay Heritage Museum: 104
Henry Ridout: 109
Wally Crowdis: 111
Marie Bisson: 114
Donell Beaton: 126
The MacDougall family: 129

Linda MacDonald: 130
Jim McNeil: 132

Beaton Institute, Cape Breton University:
Page 18 – John B. Croak, awarded the Victoria Cross, 1918. Unknown photographer. 84-1341-15441.
Page 28 – Lithograph of miners at Caledonia Gallery, 1882. Unknown artist. 81-1154-6234.
Page 32 – No. 3 Colliery, 1901. Unknown photgrapher. 80-17-4197.
Page 36 – Last pit pony in Colliery No. 26, date unknown. Owen Fitzgerald. 82-81-6781.
Page 43 – Officers during 1909 strike, 1909. Unknown photographer. 78-735-2485.
Page 62 – Clarie Gillis, c. 1950. Unknown photographer. 80-8523-5033.
Page 65 – Coal strikers, c. 1945. Unknown photographer. 96-1036-27724.
Page 70 – St. Joseph's Hospital, 1938. Unknown photographer. 83-6667-13967
Page 80 – Glace Bay harbour postcard, c. 1933. Unknown publisher. 84-766-14866.
Page 81 – Sterling Pit Crossing, Glace Bay, 1902. Unknown photographer. 87-656-17186.
Page 89 – Miner's Annual Picnic S&L Railroad, c. 1920. 77-481-615
Page 95 – Town Hall and McKeen Street,1914. Valentine and Sons, 80-557-4737 p.313
Page 99 – Main Street, date unknown. Valentine and Sons. 77-90-225 p.113
Page 101 – Glace Bay tavern, c. 1920. 80-1-4181.
Page 102 – Fishing—Glace Bay harbour, c. 1930s. Unknown photographer. 97-625-28473.
Page 108 – Glace Bay Athletic Club Firemen, c. 1920. 77-908-1042.
Page 123 – Cast in Gaelic play at the Dreamland Theatre, Glace Bay, c.1900. 77-650-784.
Page 135 – Glace Bay Commercial Street, c. 1910. 78-971-2821.
Page 137 – Glace Bay Gazette, 1945. National Film Board of Canada. 96-1029-27717.

Library and Archives Canada:

Page 58 – "Capt. Lawren P. Harris, official war artist, sketching. During World War II." Canada Dept. of National Defence/PA116593

Page 96 –"Commercial Street, Glace Bay, N.S." Albertype Company fonds/PA-032633